THE KISSING BRIDGE

ALSO BY TRICIA GOYER

The Seven Brides for Seven Bachelors series
The Memory Jar
The Promise Box

A Christmas Gift for Rose

Seeds of Love novella included in *An Amish Garden*

THE KISSING BRIDGE

THE KISSING BRIDGE

TRICIA GOYER

≣ZONDERVAN®

ZONDERVAN

The Kissing Bridge

Copyright © 2014 by Tricia Goyer

This title is also available as a Zondervan ebook. Visit www.zondervan.com/ebooks.

Requests for information should be addressed to:

Zondervan, Grand Rapids, Michigan 49530

Library of Congress Cataloging-in-Publication Data

Goyer, Tricia.

The kissing bridge / Tricia Goyer.

pages cm.

ISBN 978-0-310-33515-3 (trade paper)

1. Dating (Social customs)—Fiction. I. Title.

PS3607.O94K57 2014

813'.6—dc23

2013047068

Scripture quotations noted as NLT are taken from the *Holy Bible*, New Living Translation, copyright © 1996, 2004, 2007 by Tyndale House Foundation. Used by permission of Tyndale House Publishers, Inc., Carol Stream, Illinois 60188. All rights reserved.

Printed in the United States of America

14 15 16 17 /RRD/ 20 19 18 17 16 15 14 13 12 11 10 9 8 7 6 5 4 3 2 1

There are two people whose experiences inspired this novel.

Geneva Holmgrem.
Your passion to save lives after a harrowing experience inspired
Rebecca's character.

Cory Goyer.
Seeing you in logger sports inspired Gideon's character.
True-to-life characters come from inspiring people!

This is what the Lord says:
"Stop at the crossroads and look around.
　　Ask for the old, godly way, and walk in it.
Travel its path, and you will find rest for your souls.
　　But you reply, 'No, that's not the road we want!'"

JEREMIAH 6:16 NLT

Glossary

ab im kopp—off in the head
ach—oh
aeman—amen
aenti—aunt
appenditlich—delicious
Bann—ban
bruder—brother
danki—thanks
dat—father
dawdi—grandparent
dawdi house—grandparent's house
dumm—foolish
Es dutt mir leed—I am sorry
fraa—wife
gestalt—unity
gut—good
ja—yes
kapp—prayer cap
kumme—come
lecherich—ridiculous
liebling—darling
mem—mother
nava hucker—side sitter

oma—grandmother
opa—grandfather
voll schpaas—very funny
wunderbar—wonderful

CHAPTER

1

Her *bruder*'s soft whimper just outside the bedroom door alerted Rebecca Troyer to Claude's injury. She threw the door open to find Claude standing there with tousled hair, flecks of straw from head to toe, and a rumpled shirt. Tears made clean trails down dirty cheeks. He held up his finger to show blood seeping from a small gash.

Rebecca stepped out into the hallway onto the whitewashed wooden floor. "Whatcha do this time?" She knelt beside her seven-year-old *bruder* and sighed. He'd not only cut himself, he'd also torn the sleeve of the new shirt Mem had just sewn for him. Mending that would be more work for Mem, especially since Rebecca was leaving today. Guilt piled upon her shoulders as an invisible weight.

"I was trying to get the mama cat." Claude's large brown eyes fixed on hers. "Her kittens were crying, and she needed to feed them. The mama was up in the loft."

Compassion welled up, and Rebecca opened her arms. Claude stepped into them. She squeezed, breathing in the scent of boyish sweat and barn, and tears rimmed the edges of her eyelids.

Her lips parted slightly, but no words emerged. *I'm going to miss you, Claude.*

She wished she could speak those words and tell him she'd be back someday. Back with a degree—with knowledge—and their whole community the better for it.

Claude whimpered and pulled back slightly, and she squeezed his shoulders tighter, knowing it was one of the last hugs she'd be giving him for a while.

She released him, pushing him back to where she could get a good look at him. Her gaze narrowed. Her brow folded with sternness. "You didn't get up on that rickety ladder again, did ya?"

Claude's bottom lip puckered and trembled. "*Ja*, but the kittens' cries were so loud . . . they needed their mama."

Did the kittens' cries make him think of his own loss?

Claude had lost a mother. She'd lost a sister. Her mother had lost her older daughter and had gained a baby to care for. All on the same day. And not many months later, when Claude's young father admitted he couldn't raise the child alone, Rebecca's parents adopted their grandson, making him their son.

The day of her sister's death had also started Rebecca on her path to leaving the Amish. Not even her parents knew she was going. If they did, there was no way they'd let her go. And so she'd been lying to them for years, talking about Amish boys in the community who'd caught her fancy and about getting baptized next fall, all the while figuring out how to escape.

The ache she carried inside from longing for her sister—Claude's mother—urged her on.

Rebecca placed a soft hand on Claude's shoulder.

"That ol' barn cat won't let her kittens go hungry. You don't need to worry about that." She stood straighter, forcing sternness. "You need to obey Dat. Listen to him. He's jest watchin' out for your safety. Disobedience will only hurt you, ya hear?" She straightened her shoulders and fingered the string of her *kapp*. "Now go find Mem and ask her for a bandage."

Claude's eyes widened, and his jaw dropped. "But—but . . . you always do it."

"*Ja*, when I'm here. But what do you do when I'm at work? You know I'm not always going to be here, don't ya?" Moistness filled her eyes again, but she quickly blinked it away. "I can hear Mem downstairs getting the last of things together for *Aenti*'s birthday party. Go on now."

Claude held his finger closer to her, forcing her to look at the drops of blood. Rebecca took in a deep breath and jutted out her chin. "Mem will help you. I have to go to work, *ja*?"

An ache radiated from her stomach. *How can I go through with this?*

With a whimper, Claude turned and scurried back downstairs. Rebecca urged herself to stay strong—to stick to the plan.

Her hand trembled as she picked up a small hand mirror. She checked her hair and her *kapp*, then returned the mirror to the dresser top and grabbed her purse. Her suitcase was already in the trunk of Lora's car. Lora had worked at the Garden Gate Cafe with Rebecca until she realized she could make three times as much money driving the Amish. The funniest part of Lora's new job was that no one realized her father used to be Amish, or knew Lora could understand everything they said in Pennsylvania Dutch.

Rebecca grimaced. No doubt by tomorrow everyone in Shipshewana would be talking about her leaving. These things didn't take long to get around.

A truck door slammed, the noise coming from the gravel driveway outside. The sound of her older *bruder* getting dropped off from his factory job told Rebecca she only had a few minutes to make it outside to the road before Lora arrived. She grabbed her sweater from the hook on the wall and hurried down the hallway, nearly jogging down the stairs to the first floor. In the kitchen, Mem bandaged Claude's finger. Rebecca wished she could walk over and give her mother a solid hug like she used to do as a child, but Mem would then know for certain that something was wrong. Instead Rebecca offered them a quick wave.

"Headin' out?" Mem called, pausing Rebecca's steps.

Rebecca turned, clutching her purse to her chest. "*Ja*, Lora should be here any moment."

Mem's eyebrows folded. "But I thought Wednesdays were your day off." She set the box of bandages on the table and took a step in Rebecca's direction. Claude whimpered but didn't say a word.

Rebecca shrugged. "*Ja, vell*, change of plans." She swallowed hard, hoping her emotions didn't show. Heat rose to her cheeks.

Mem's gaze fixed on her. "Is everything all right? You haven't been yourself lately."

"*Ja*, I'm fine. Everything's fine." She wanted to tell her mem that she hadn't been herself since Claude's birth—since her sister's death—but Rebecca held her tongue. The matter was in God's hands. Rebecca just wished her pain and missin' were in His hands too.

"Will you be home late?" Mem hurriedly asked. "We will miss you at the party. Didn't you have to work last year on your aunt's birthday too?"

"I, uh, can't remember, but I'll be home at the regular time. Don't wait up for me." *And don't feel as if any of this was your fault*, she wanted to add. The letter she'd left, tucked into the top of her trunk, would explain everything.

Rebecca hurried out the front door before she changed her mind. Her eyes scanned the roadway, and she spotted Lora's white Buick approaching. Afternoon light glimmered off the freshly washed car, and Rebecca's heart sank. Lora only washed the car when she had a full day of taxiing. Even though the Amish didn't believe in being prideful, for some reason those in the community always called drivers with the nicest, cleanest cars first.

Rebecca's light-gray sweater hung over her arm, and her simple purse dangled from her shoulder. The autumn day was warm, but she refused to enjoy it. Refused to take one last look back at her parents' farm.

She half walked and half jogged toward the road as Lora slowed the car and pulled in the driveway. Rebecca hid her disappointment to see Fannie Petershwim sitting in the front seat, with her daughter Karen sitting in the backseat. Rebecca glared at Lora through the side window, and Lora offered the slightest of shrugs, as if to say, "A paying job is a paying job."

Lora hadn't asked for money for all the rides she'd given Rebecca over the years. Rebecca had no right to complain. Every once in a while she'd baked something nice for her friend, and had often wished she could do more. Now she wished she could offer to fill Lora's gas tank, but Rebecca needed every penny for her future—for the journey ahead.

Rebecca slid into the backseat and caught Fannie in the middle of a conversation with her daughter. "Maybe she has extra time on her hands with her two youngest leaving the Amish. They both got jobs up in Grand Rapids, but that'll bring only harm. I just hope their dat will be able to keep up with all the work on his farm alone. He might have to hire it out, although I don't know how you can support a family doing that yet."

Ten minutes later Shipshewana loomed ahead, but the woman's mouth never slowed. Fannie didn't talk to Lora, and she'd barely acknowledged Rebecca. Butterflies fluttered in Rebecca's stomach. If this was how neighbors treated her, what could she expect from strangers . . . from the world? Yet even being alone was better than that feeling of helplessness when she'd watched her sister's soul slip into eternity without being able to do one thing about it.

Rebecca straightened her shoulders and pressed back against the seat, staring out the side window as the first stores of Shipshewana came into view.

Never again.

Caleb Hooley lifted the ax and swung with all his might, feeling the satisfaction of the sharpened metal sinking deep into the wood of the pine tree in front of him.

He wiped the sweat off his brow with the back of his hand and glanced at Amos Byler. "Okay, let's see how long it takes you to dig that ax out of the tree." Though his friend was two inches shorter, Amos had the tenacity of Red Gerald's mule—Red Gerald being the closest neighbor to their bachelor cabin—and Caleb liked that. He was thankful to find a friend in West Kootenai who would accept his challenges. Life was too short to play it safe—to tend one's horses and muck one's stalls and lose out on all the heart-pumping parts of life. If his *opa* had taught him anything, it was that.

Amos walked over to the tall tree and wrapped two hands around the ax handle. Then, planting his right foot on the tree trunk, he yanked with all his might. His face reddened, and Caleb chuckled under his breath.

It was a beautiful evening in West Kootenai, Montana. They'd made progress on the guesthouse they were building over at Abe and Ruth Sommer's place, and now this evening they'd reverted back to their own version of logger sports. Rumor had it the Sommer family was making the cabin extra nice so that when their son and daughter-in-law came to visit from back east, they just might want to stay. But Caleb only listened and nodded to the rumors buzzing around West Kootenai Kraft and Grocery. He'd rather beat his time climbing the tall tree behind their cabin than consider who was going to move here and all their motives behind that decision. *Woman talk.*

Caleb looked around as Amos tugged at the ax with grunts and groans. High mountain peaks rose on the horizon. Tall larch and pine trees filled the air with a glorious aroma. Just yesterday he'd seen a brown bear cub splashing in the creek, and this morning a wild turkey had made all sort of ruckus on the front porch of the bachelors' cabin, as if daring them to get up and chase him.

And then there were the other bachelors. They'd all moved here in early spring so they'd be eligible for their resident hunting license in the fall. In Montana, they could hunt the big game—bear, elk, moose, even mountain goats. And hunting season was only a few months away.

For this year, at least, he could hang out with his friends, embark on all sorts of adventures, shoot guns and practice with crossbows, without having to think about tending a farm, dealing with family issues back at his parents' place, or even worrying about who would be a good wife.

Not that he was against marrying. There was still time. He was only twenty-three, and it would happen someday, he supposed. For as long as Caleb could remember, he liked the idea of having a wife and being able to kiss her anytime he wanted.

"Pull harder, Amos!" Caleb called, knowing his mem would have a heart attack to see him competing in such a manner. Back home in Ohio they weren't even allowed to play competitive ball games in the school yard, lest they become prideful in their competition. Here, he thrived on it—just as long as they were out of view of the stricter Amish folk in their community.

Amos grunted and tugged again. They were both surprised when the ax broke free. As if in slow motion, Amos' body flew back and the ax sailed through the air, flipping over Amos' head, heading straight for Caleb's leg. He jumped back just in time. The ax hit the ground with a thud.

Laughter poured from Caleb's lips. "Almost got double points with that one—for the release and the bull's-eye."

Amos held the back of his head and moaned. "*Ja*, then you better add in a few more points for the knot on the back of my skull—war injury."

Without hesitation, Amos jumped to his feet, picked up the ax, and eyed the tree. He glanced back at Caleb, and then he swung as high as he could, hitting the trunk. The loud thud proved the ax dug deep. Caleb rolled up his sleeves and stepped forward—ready to accept any challenge that was sent his way.

So far Montana hadn't offered up anything—anyone—he'd consider his match.

CHAPTER

2

Rebecca breathed a sigh of relief as Fannie and her daughter exited the car, heading into Lolly's Fabric Store. After quickly scanning the street—to make sure there wasn't anyone she knew—Rebecca moved from the backseat to the front, pulling off her *kapp* and placing it in the seat between her and Lora.

She wrapped one arm around her stomach and nibbled on the thumbnail of her opposite hand. "Did you happen to check the train schedule on the Internet to see if everything's running on time?"

Lora checked her side-view mirror and then pulled out. "Did you run out of data minutes on your phone again?" Excitement tinged Lora's voice. Over the last two months she'd been talking about the cross-country trip. She'd looked over the Amtrak schedules maybe more than Rebecca had. The truth was, not many people left LaGrange County. And when folks did, they rarely returned.

Like Marianna.

"*Ja*, all my minutes are gone." Rebecca pushed thoughts of Marianna out of her mind. Marianna was married now—to an

Englischer. The last thing Rebecca needed was to add trouble to herself by visiting her shunned friend. It would be bad enough when her parents discovered what she'd left to do.

Lora chuckled. "You used all your minutes sending Facebook messages to some handsome stranger, yes?"

"I wish." Rebecca sighed. "Nothing quite as exciting as that. Do you know how hard it was to take an anatomy test on a tiny screen on my phone? Thankfully, it was just a multiple-choice test that went with last week's lab."

Lora gasped as if horrified. "You're just a rebel, Rebecca. Sneaking a phone . . . and taking *college classes.*" She sighed and shook her head. "My parents would buy me my own top-of-the-line computer if I was half as interested in school as you are. Do your parents know yet?"

"*Ne.*" She lowered her head, fiddling with the snaps on her sweater. "They're at *Aenti* Mary Sue's birthday party tonight. They most likely won't even know I'm gone until tomorrow morning when I don't come to breakfast. They're used to me coming in late."

"But you told them what you're doing—where you're going—in the letter that you wrote them, right?"

"*Vell* . . ." Rebecca glanced at the passenger's-side window, resisting the urge to wave as they passed the buggy of an older couple her family knew. "I told them in the letter that I was going to Oregon. I didn't mention college. Just writing that I was leaving was difficult enough. I didn't want to break their hearts twice in the same note."

"It's *just* college," Lora urged. "And you're doing it to help people—help those in your own community. Help make sure that what happened to Claudia won't happen again."

A lump rose in Rebecca's throat, and she tried to swallow it away. "I want to help, all right, but I don't know if I'll ever be able to do it in my own community. I can maybe go somewhere people don't know me as well, like Goshen or Napsee . . . and then maybe work with the Mennonites with hopes they will help me to educate their Amish friends." Rebecca's fists tightened into two balls on her lap. "Your dad was Amish, Lora. You know that's not how things work. You can't join the church and then run off to college and get an education. And I don't know anyone who's come back from college and joined the church. College is 'the world' . . . It's just not their way."

Lora released a slow breath and turned onto the county highway. "Oh, yeah, it makes total sense to me. Let's let more people in our community die—that's better than allowing someone to become educated by the world, *ja*?"

Rebecca didn't answer. What was the use? Her family— her community—trusted that everything, especially life and death, was in the hands of God. But couldn't this desire deep within her to be a nurse be from Him too? She wanted to think so, but she doubted her parents would agree.

Her *oma* used to say that God created each person for His own good purpose. Something inside her heart told Rebecca that her purpose was to help women live better, longer lives through nursing. But how could that be from God if she had to walk away from His people and her family to follow Him?

Rebecca didn't want to think about it anymore. She'd gotten very little sleep lately asking the same questions. She instead turned her attention to Lora.

"So how did that date with Chad turn out—wasn't that his name?"

Lora bit her lower lip. "Oh, well, it was fine, I guess." Red heat moved up her neck. "He's really nice, and he treated me well. He bought dinner and even brought flowers."

"*Ja*, 'jest fine'? Your face says it's more than 'jest fine.'"
Even as Rebecca teased her friend, a longing welled up in her
chest. What she wouldn't give to feel the same excitement . . .
There had been a few Amish young men she'd been attracted
to, but she hadn't let herself explore her feelings. Why should
she when she'd planned on leaving?

Lora glanced over and winked. "I won't kiss and tell."

Rebecca sighed. "I jest wish I had something to tell about."

"You've had plenty of offers of dates, Rebecca. I heard it
from Elmina Yoder's own mouth that her son Monroe was
quite upset when he showed up at your house and you wouldn't
let him in the front door."

Rebecca pouted out her lower lip. "I like Monroe all right.
He's fine enough. I just couldn't do it to him, to anyone."

"Do what?"

"Shame him. Love 'em and leave 'em. Make him the
laughingstock of the community when his girlfriend leaves to
pursue her education."

"Good decision." Lora turned the car onto the road leading
to Elkhart. "You don't want to waste your heart, your emotions, on someone who's 'jest fine.' I've made that mistake."

"*Ja*, but how will I know when the right one comes?"
Rebecca asked.

"You'll feel it from your nose to your toes. You'll get all
heated up as if you've just been attacked by fire ants."

Rebecca chuckled, playing along. "Why, that sounds jest
horrible!"

Lora waved a hand. "I'd like something so terrible to bite
me." She winked. "I have a feeling, Rebecca, that once you get
out of this suffocating community your heart will have a chance
to open up. Let it." Lora reached over and patted Rebecca's
arm. "Promise me you'll let it."

"I can't promise that, Lora." Rebecca shrugged with about as much enthusiasm as Claude had when told to get ready for a bath. "I'm not leaving the community to find a boyfriend. I'm leaving for an education, and that is that."

Lora nodded but didn't say a word. She didn't understand. Rebecca didn't expect her to.

Fifteen minutes later, Lora parked the car and climbed out. Rebecca used the mirror on the sun visor to return her *kapp* to her head. She didn't have time to change out of her Amish clothes, and it would be disrespectful to wear the clothes without her *kapp*. When the train was under way, she could change into her *Englisch* clothes from her suitcase.

A strange sensation came over her as she realized this was probably the last time she'd wear Amish clothes . . . at least for a while. She wouldn't wear them in Oregon. Her plan was to fit in. To do her work without being noticed. She felt sadness, mixed with regret, that life couldn't have been simpler. It wasn't that she wanted to leave or rebel. She simply didn't have a choice—not if she was going to follow what she knew in her heart was right.

Where would I be if Claudia hadn't died?

Maybe she'd be sharing kisses with a handsome Amish guy and promising not to kiss and tell. The worst part was that God could have changed everything. He could have saved Claudia. Wasn't that what her parents had raised her to believe: that God had the power to create the storm and to still the wind?

No . . . don't think of that. Anger bubbled inside, but she pushed it down. She couldn't stay mad at God. Not now. He was the only One boarding that train with her.

Lora popped open the car's trunk, and Rebecca hurried to the back of the car and pulled out her suitcase. Her whole world was encased within the old, brown-leather satchel she'd picked up at Goodwill.

They walked toward the door of the station. Rebecca paused before going inside. "You don't have to come. I know that you have things to do."

Lora offered a sad smile. "Are you kidding? This is a big step. I'm not going to send you off alone."

"That's kind of you. But it's really not necessary."

"So that's it? You're leaving cross-country, and you're not going to let a soul see you off?"

How could Rebecca tell her friend that she didn't want to cry . . . and seeing Lora on the platform would cause her to do just that.

"*Danki,* but really, I'll be fine." The suitcase pulled down her arm. Around her, people moved to and from the train station. They parted around the two friends like water flowing around rocks in a stream. "I'll write and give you my address when I'm settled. I want you to write to me about Chad, you hear? Don't leave any detail out . . . Well, except for the mushy details."

"*Ja* . . ." Lora smiled, using her Pennsylvania Dutch. She looked as if she was going to offer a hug, but then took a step back. "Oh, one more thing. I have your mail."

"*Ach, gut.* I forgot about that." Rebecca grabbed the envelopes and tucked them into her purse. She'd used Lora's address for all her school bills and college correspondence. The last thing she needed was a report card showing up at her parents' house, especially when they thought she divided her time between selling cupcakes at the bakery and hanging out with friends, both of which were more acceptable in their eyes.

Ten minutes later she was seated on the train. She clung to the handle of her suitcase, thankful she had been able to trust

Lora not to look inside it. Her future depended on what the leather suitcase contained.

She refused to look out the window as the train squealed and moaned, rolling to a start.

She was doing this for children just like Claude, she reminded herself. No child should have to grow up without a mother, and even though she'd been helpless once . . . Never again. Even if it meant sacrificing her future, her hopes of marriage, and—according to her Amish beliefs—her soul, more than anything she wanted to be a nurse.

Rebecca held her breath, amazed she was really doing this. She was the only Amish person in a nearly full train car. Butterflies ping-ponged in her stomach as her seat rocked to the rhythm of the rumbling passenger car. The scents of perfume, potato chips, and cigarettes made her stomach rumble even more. Thankfully, no one sat beside her. They saw her as different. What would they think when she returned from the restroom in *Englisch* clothes? Would they even care?

Only when the town of Elkhart was far out of view did she look at her mail. *Bill. Bill. Information about on-campus housing. Ach . . . a letter from Marianna.*

Rebecca ripped open the envelope.

Dear Rebecca, dearest friend,

Danki for giving me Lora's address. I didn't know how your parents would respond if they saw a note from your wayward friend in their mailbox. I haven't written to many people lately. When I do, I either don't hear back or I get back impersonal letters that quote Scripture about the mistakes they believe I made in marrying Ben. Even my circle-letter friends are writing about how they are worried about my soul. But if they really believe that, what good do their words do? By their own confession there is no hope for me. I'm no longer part of the Amish community, and I'm married to an Englischer. I made my choice. And even if it is possible for a divorced person to be part of the Amish community, I love my husband with all my heart.

Listen to me, babbling so. Danki, friend, for listening. You've always been there, and I don't think I've appreciated it enough. I have friends here, but it's not the same. There's something special about having someone who can remember the first pie you tried to bake together. (I've never mixed up salt and sugar since then, thank goodness.) Also something special about a friend who listened endlessly to me talking about the boy who sat in back of me in school. And the friend who knocked out my first baby tooth with her elbow. Ach, writing this has made me miss you so. I wish you'd head out west sometime. I'd love the look in your eyes seeing the bear scat just beyond my back porch!

Well, it's not going to be a long letter today. My friend Millie Arnold asked me to walk with her to the lake. She's sixty-six years old. She was a rancher's wife before her husband passed away, and she's in better shape than me. I come home from our walks winded . . . not only from the exercise, but from the laughter.

Ach, I see her approaching. I better get my tennis shoes laced up!

Love, Marianna

Rebecca sighed. She couldn't help but smile, thinking about her friend. Marianna had found what every Amish woman dreamed of: a man who loved her, a good home. And the next natural step would be to start a family. Tension tightened in Rebecca's gut. How far was West Kootenai from good health care? Was there a good midwife in the area? A doctor? The worries plagued her, clacking in her brain like the wheels on the tracks.

After a few minutes, she tucked Marianna's letter into her purse and then pulled out the train schedule Lora had printed out for her. Her finger followed the train tracks through the states and into Montana. She sucked in a breath to see that their path took the train through Whitefish. Somewhere in her memory she remembered Marianna telling her that it was the closest train station to West Kootenai—only an hour away from the community where Marianna lived.

Rebecca's heart skipped a beat. Why hadn't she thought of this before? She didn't start classes for over a month. She could visit Marianna—at least for a few weeks. Marianna had invited her to come, hadn't she?

Rebecca pulled her cell phone from her purse and noticed the woman across the aisle staring. Rebecca looked away, focusing outside the window at the golden fields the train passed by. The woman hadn't seemed interested that she was Amish until she saw her cell phone. Rebecca dialed, and when Marianna didn't answer, she left a message for her friend to call her and then tucked the phone back into her purse. If Rebecca had learned one thing, it was that people believed the worst kind of Amish woman was one who didn't give the appearance of humility and simplicity that everyone thought she should. Who used a phone or even a computer for her job.

She was just glad that after she changed her clothes today, she would no longer have to straddle two worlds. She could be a nursing student, not an Amish woman, and no one would be the wiser for it.

CHAPTER

3

It was nearly dark as Caleb and Amos headed back to the bachelors' cabin. Their steps, a staccato of heavy crunches, carried through the forest. The ground was littered with broken branches, dried brush, and pinecones. In a matter of months it would all be frosted with white snow—a thick layer, he hoped, like on Mem's cinnamon rolls. With the snow it was easier to walk quietly through the forest, but now . . . Every sound echoed and bounced through the trees.

"Hear anything?" Amos asked.

Caleb paused to listen. "*Ne.*"

"It's the sound of my breaking heart. I was hoping to find someone to take on a date Saturday night, but there aren't any young women in these parts who aren't taken."

"There are a few." Caleb smirked.

"Do you have your eye on one?"

"Nah, I haven't found anyone yet with a little sense of adventure." Adventure was the one thing that had been on his mind since he'd been in Montana. Adventure was what he'd come for. It was his grandfather's dying wish—for Caleb to explore the world as his grandfather never had. He'd made a promise, after all.

"You could have gone on that hike with us—up to Mount Robinson this spring," Amos said.

"Going on a hike once a year doesn't make someone an adventurous person. Is it too much to think there is a woman who cares about something else other than quilting or gardening?"

"You *are* looking for an Amish woman, *ja*? What you ask for is *lecherich*."

Caleb swallowed hard. He turned to Amos and studied his face in the dimming light. Amos' cheeks were red from exertion. His friend lifted his eyebrows, waiting for a response.

"*Ja, ja, lecherich,* ridiculous, of course." What else could he say? Yes, he wanted to stay Amish. He just couldn't imagine spending the rest of his life living by a normal routine. One's days were short. Life went by too fast. His *opa* had taught him that.

He'd been eager to come to Montana for adventure, but what would happen when he returned home was never far from his thoughts. Wasn't there more—something that really mattered, that he could do beyond following the cycle of the seasons and living a farmer's life?

Back at their cabin, they made a quick dinner. Afterward Caleb took his harmonica out to the front porch. He turned it over in his fingers. He guessed it had once been silver, but the sides were now worn bronze. As he rocked in a chair on the front porch, he imagined his grandfather's fingerprints ingrained there from all the nights of playing.

To Caleb the sound of the harmonica ushered in spring and carried through fall. It was as naturally a part of the seasons as the blooms of nature and birth of new creatures.

Only winter was silent with the still of the snow, the cold of the air, and the harmonica tucked in his *opa*'s dresser drawer until the sight of the first robin. For as much as *Opa* had enjoyed playing, *Oma* insisted that it be played outside. Some Amish communities, she reminded them, didn't allow harmonicas to be played at all. And now . . . Caleb played in his stead. Yet he would do anything to be sitting at his grandfather's side listening to *Opa* play. If one could only turn back time . . .

Caleb's gut ached, and he wished he'd taken time to ask *Opa* how to play more tunes. But while he didn't have variety, he had heart and now played a favorite hymn as he stared up at an inky, star-studded sky. Usually there was the hoot of an owl or the rustling of a raccoon, but not tonight. It was as if all the animals stilled to listen to his hymn.

He'd first heard about the West Kootenai area from copies of the *Budget* that he'd read to *Opa* during the last three years as he lost his vision. The *Budget* writers talked about hunting and bears in their yards and moose sightings and snow as high as a front door. Reading about it, Caleb knew he had to get there one day for a visit. The only problem was, he didn't have the right woman to share this adventure with. There were a few nice single girls in West Kootenai, but no one he could offer his heart to.

His dat had scolded him years ago when he refused to take Joan Sutter on a second date. "Kissin' wears out, cookin' doesn't," Dat had declared. Yet as much as he enjoyed a good meal, Caleb hoped that one day he'd find a woman with a bit of spunk, who didn't mind a little adventure now and then, and who'd hopefully have a twinkle of humor peering up at him from wide eyes beneath her *kapp*. Was that too much to ask?

He finished his hymn and then made his way back into

the cabin. Amos sat up from his bunk as Caleb entered. He pointed to the countertop cluttered with coffee mugs, newspapers, bullets, bits of rope, and rolls of duct tape.

"There's another letter from your mem," Amos said.

"*Ja*, thanks for picking that up for me."

"Aren't you going to read them? I think there's at least two months' worth that you haven't touched."

Caleb shrugged. "It's just the same old news from home. How exciting can harvesting wheat be? And who cares which neighbor secretly has a cell phone with Facebook?" He tried to keep his tone light. "I'm certain my mem is just trying to do her part in keeping in contact. Maybe tomorrow I'll write a postcard to let her know I'm busy working and such."

He reached back and rubbed the back of his neck. Just seeing those letters caused his shoulders to knot up, tightening down like his parents' windup clock on the mantel.

Amos didn't look convinced. How could Caleb explain that Mem's words broke his heart over and over again? He didn't want to know how hard it was on everyone since Grandpa's stroke. He didn't want to face the fact that he'd walked away from the farm when his family needed him most. His promise to his grandfather kept him in the West Kootenai despite that.

Caleb turned off their kerosene lamp and glanced at Amos, giving him a good-night nod. He thought about wishing his friend sweet dreams, but what was the use? No matter how good one's dreams, the reality was that the death of someone as wonderful as his *opa* was a part of life. It meant saying good-bye before you were ready and not being able to breathe as the words escaped.

Somewhere between St. Paul and St. Cloud, Minnesota, Rebecca got ahold of Marianna on the phone. Instead of her Amish dress, she'd changed into a simple skirt and blouse. Her *kapp* was tucked into her satchel too.

"Rebecca, I'm so glad that you called. I was surprised to hear your voice on my voice mail. It was a pleasant surprise." Her friend's voice echoed through the phone. How many nights had they shared a bed during sleepovers, talking late into the night about their futures? Rebecca never could have imagined Marianna leaving the Amish. And even more, she never would have imagined she would be too.

Rebecca pulled her sweater tighter around her. The air was cooler than she liked on the train. Or maybe it was the sound of Marianna's voice that had caused goose bumps to rise on her arms.

"I was wondering if I could visit. I've missed seeing you, and I would love to see Ben again. And your parents. Is everyone doing well?"

"*Ja*, everyone is *gut*." Marianna's voice slipped easily back into Pennsylvania Dutch. "Mem and Dat are having a guesthouse built. They're hoping Levi and Naomi will come for a spell. They are so excited to see baby Samuel. And speaking of excitement, I'd love for you to come! It would be *wunderbar*. Do you have a date in mind?"

"*Ja*, sort of." Rebecca chuckled. "And it might be a little sooner than you expect. I was thinking about tomorrow."

"Tomorrow? Do you mean you'll be leaving Indiana tomorrow?"

"*Ne*, I mean I'll be arriving tomorrow. The truth is . . . I'm already on the train."

The clacking of the train wheels on the track rang out, but only silence came from the phone.

"I did wonder what that noise was. Is everything all right?" Marianna finally asked. "Are you . . . in trouble?"

"Trouble? *Ne.*" She pushed the words out. "I mean things are *gut* with my family. I'm not running from any trouble." She chuckled, trying to keep the conversation light.

"*Ja*, well, that's *gut*. After Naomi turned up pregnant . . . Well, I'm sorry that I even asked. It's a wonderful surprise that you're coming. I just never expected it would really happen. And tomorrow . . ." Marianna's voice bubbled through the phone. "I'm excited for you to see our new place. Ben built me a cabin. He tells me it's family size. I'm excited that you'll be our first guest. You do have a chaperone with you, right?"

"Just me. But I'll explain when I get there."

"*Ja*, I understand . . ." From Marianna's voice, it was clear she didn't really understand. "I just doubt I'll be able to sleep a wink until you do," she added.

It wasn't common, they both knew, for a young Amish woman to travel alone, and Rebecca had no doubt Marianna would be up all night worrying about her and praying for her. Rebecca wished she could explain now, but it wasn't something she could talk about over the phone. The tears would come when she did. Tears she didn't want the other passengers witnessing.

Rebecca gave Marianna the time of arrival in Whitefish and then told her friend she'd see her tomorrow. Even as she hung up the phone, a new excitement lightened her heart. For many years she'd silently focused on what she'd be leaving. Now—for the first time—she was excited by who was waiting for her across the miles. If anyone would understand her leaving, it had to be Marianna.

Rebecca did her best to sleep on the train, but instead she found herself counting down the hours to Whitefish. She was eager to see a friendly face. Eager to spill her heart to someone who knew her—really knew her. She also couldn't wait to see Marianna without her Amish clothes. Rebecca couldn't picture such a thing. If she'd had to guess which friend would live far from LaGrange County, which one would turn in her *kapp* for a chap, Marianna would have been her last choice.

On the train most people kept to themselves. Rebecca passed the time talking to an older woman who was on the way to Spokane to see her daughter. The woman talked to Rebecca with an ease that Rebecca wasn't used to. In her Amish dress people were usually hesitant to talk to her, as if it wasn't allowed. Or worse, as if Rebecca was an oddity. But in her *Englisch* clothes she felt different—like a new person.

It was a feeling Rebecca didn't like very much. Yet this was what she wanted . . . wasn't it? Wasn't this what she'd been working so hard for?

Before Rebecca knew it, the train was pulling into Whitefish. She gasped at the view outside the window of the mountains, the tall pine trees, and the blue sky that stretched farther than she'd ever seen.

She rose and moved toward the train door as the train slowed, holding on to the door rail as the train came to a stop. Her free hand clung to her suitcase. When the conductor opened the door, a fresh, warm breeze blew in.

She stepped off the train, and her stomach growled at the aroma of barbecue beef somewhere close by. Soon both feet were planted on asphalt, but she remained silent, still—trying to get her bearings. She was in Montana. She had left home. Her parents had no idea where she was . . .

Yet even here there was a familiar face. Marianna stood at the end of the walkway that led to the train station. She wasn't wearing Amish clothes, but the skirt, blouse, and head scarf were simple. Similar to the clothes Rebecca had chosen, minus the head scarf. One could leave the Amish with her actions, but it was clear Marianna still held tight to some traditions with her heart. Rebecca did too.

Marianna's eyes scanned the passengers. Rebecca shuffled slightly. She should have warned her friend that she wouldn't be wearing Amish dress. Marianna passed over her twice, and then her eyes finally paused. Her eyebrows lifted in surprise. Rebecca self-consciously brushed a strand of dark hair off her shoulder and then smiled and waved.

She hesitantly walked forward, suitcase in hand, but it was Marianna who rushed to her, arms wide open. She paused before Rebecca and pulled her into a hug.

"Look at you! You're here."

"*Ja*, I have a hard time believing it myself."

"You'll have to tell me more . . . about, uh, everything." Marianna eyed Rebecca's blouse and skirt. "And excuse me if I stare. I didn't realize my closest friend had such a cute figure. *Englisch* clothes?"

Rebecca blushed. "*Ja*, there is much to tell." She readjusted her suitcase in her hand and then scanned the busy sidewalks around the train station. "Is Ben here? I'd love to see him again. When he was back in Shipshe, well, his mind was on other things than visiting your friends and neighbors. Not that my family would have welcomed him in if he had *kumme* visiting."

"That's the truth. Everyone in the community was leery of him . . . and I can see that their concerns weren't unfounded."

Pink tinged Marianna's cheeks. She shifted her weight from one foot to another. "But *es dutt mir leed* . . . I'm sorry that he couldn't make it. They had their last day of filming his newest music video." Marianna glanced at her watch. "I left early this morning to get some shopping done in Kalispell. The video shoot will probably be done by the time we get there. We can have lunch at my house. I have a pot of soup on, if that's all right . . . unless you need something sooner?"

"Later is fine. I ate on the train." She didn't tell Marianna that she'd nibbled on Mem's oatmeal cookies for a day and a half. She just hoped Dat forgave her for stealing them out of the cookie jar and tucking them into her purse the evening before she left.

They walked around the side of the building to the parking lot. The day was sunny and warm, and children played on an old train engine that had been set up on the grass for a display.

Rebecca scanned the parking lot, looking for a driver. "I forgot to tell you over the phone that I'd be happy to pay for the driver too. I know it's a long way."

Marianna approached a large blue truck and pulled out a key from her skirt pocket. "*Ach*, I don't have a driver. Ben taught me to drive, and I got my license three months ago."

"You . . . drive?" Rebecca paused in her steps. She looked around the side of the truck, almost expecting someone to jump out and yell, "Surprise!"

"*Ja*. I didn't think it would fluster you so."

Rebecca heard the doors unlock, and she opened hers. "I'm, uh, not flustered."

Marianna got into the driver's seat and then cast a glance in Rebecca's direction. "Remember who you're talking to here. You're not going to be able to pull much wool over my eyes, Becks."

Rebecca set her suitcase in the backseat of the truck and then got in. "Wow, I haven't heard that name in a while."

"You don't mind, do you? I'm not sure why that name came to me all of a sudden . . ." Marianna started the truck, and the roar of the engine caused Rebecca to jump. She'd seen large trucks like this in Indiana, but she'd never ridden in one—especially one driven by someone who'd spent her whole life being transported by horse and buggy.

Her heartbeat quickened, but it had little to do with Marianna's driving. Hearing her childhood nickname, a hundred memories flooded in.

"No, but . . ." Tears came unexpectedly, and she pulled the cuff of her sweater over her palm and quickly wiped her eyes. "There were only two people who used that name. I'd almost forgotten. I haven't heard it in years."

Marianna moved to put the truck into gear and then paused. "*Ach*, I'm so sorry. I didn't mean to bring that up. I— well, I forgot that Claudia also used to call you that."

Rebecca tucked a strand of silky brown hair behind her ear and then offered a sad smile. "I'm not sure who picked it up from whom." She wanted to say more, but what? There were no words to describe her loss.

Marianna pulled out, then drove her friend around on a short tour of the downtown area of Whitefish. It looked like much hadn't changed in fifty years with the old buildings, tall facades, wagon-wide streets, and the window shoppers strolling, wearing western clothes. Soon they were on their way, heading up to the West Kootenai. As she drove, Marianna told Rebecca about the Native Americans who'd first lived in the area, about some of the first settlers, and a little about the community now.

"If you ever want to know anything about our corner of

the world, you have to ask Edgar. He's a clerk at the Kraft and Grocery, and his parents were some of the first settlers in the area. There's a big lake we're going to cross over—you'll see it. It's called Lake Koocanusa. And in the valley where the water now rests, there used to be a little town. Edgar's folks homesteaded there, and Edgar calls it *his* lake."

The two-lane road took them through beautiful country. Every now and then Rebecca would slip her camera from her purse and take a few shots of the mountains. She felt guilty every time she did. Guilty about not wearing Amish dress too. Guiltier than she thought she would feel. She'd sometimes worn these clothes around *Englisch* friends from work when she stayed at their homes, but around Marianna she'd always played the role of an Amish girl. There was so much Marianna didn't know. Even before her friend left Indiana, Rebecca had been hiding the fact that she'd been taking online classes.

As they drove, she waited for Marianna to ask about why she'd left, where she was going, and what she was planning to do, but her friend didn't comment about it. The slower pace of Montana had settled Marianna's heart in a way Rebecca had never seen. Marianna had always been gentle and sweet, but now she had a contented glow about her face that gave Rebecca the sense Marianna had found the love she'd been looking for.

Rebecca bit her lip, wishing she could claim the same. There had been little contentment and virtually no peace the last seven years. The closest feeling of satisfaction came when she'd been taking the Emergency Medical Technician class in Elkhart. She'd often traveled over on Friday nights with Lora and stayed with a friend of a friend to make it to the Saturday classes.

Rebecca had noted the disappointment in her parents'

gazes whenever she left on Fridays. She'd wanted to explain that she wasn't out partying, but the truth would bring them no comfort. Not one bit.

After about an hour, the winding road began to run alongside a lake, and a large metal bridge crossed the expanse. Rebecca sucked in a breath. The lake was deep blue and contrasted with the light-blue sky that had not even a hint of clouds. A speedboat cut a white swath through the water, leaving a foaming wake, and above it the bridge glistened as if made of silver rather than steel.

Marianna sighed. "Even though it's still another fifteen-minute drive up into the mountains, I always feel like I'm coming home when I cross the bridge."

"This place is like something from a picture book. I'm not even going to try to take a photo, because there's no way to capture it."

"It's a beautiful place, all right, and the people are even more special. When you move in, it's like becoming part of an established tribe who has your back no matter what happens."

"But that's the way it is in our Amish communities, isn't it? That's the whole point of *gestalt*, unity."

"I'm not talking about just the Amish community, but the whole community."

"Amish and *Englisch* together?" Rebecca pulled her thumbnail to her lips and bit down.

"*Ja*. And I'm talking about more than just *Englisch* drivers. In Indiana most of the community only communicates with the *Englisch* when they need to hire a driver or get help from an *Englisch* doctor, but here in West Kootenai the relationships go far beyond that. The people here consider each other friends."

Rebecca nodded. She'd heard about the Montana Amish

community, especially after the Sommer family decided to move for good. Many people said that folks moved to this area to live more liberally—to be out from under the eye of their bishops.

With the bridge behind them, Marianna turned the truck to the right and started up the dirt-and-gravel road. Rebecca looked down to the lake. Cliffs of rocks dropped straight down. Pine trees clung to the cliffs, growing outward and upward. Rebecca guessed that their roots had to go deep for them to hold on like that.

Her body rocked as the truck drove over ruts and potholes, and for the first time she questioned if she'd made a mistake coming here. Maybe that's what her family would think she was doing—leaving their community for the sake of ease of living.

Rebecca turned her head and stared out the windows at the thickening pine forests. Ease was the last thing on her mind.

"*Ja*, there is a friendship among the people who live here. We are so secluded. We need each other. If there is a fire, it takes forty-five minutes for a fire engine to come from Eureka. But there are smaller ways we help each other too . . . It's hard to explain. You're just going to have to see."

"But how can that be? Our—the Amish—community is supposed to be separate from the world."

"*Ach*, they are, in many ways. In fact, there are a lot of people who aren't happy that I left the Amish—even from this area. My *Englisch* friends accept me, of course, but I have many Amish friends who will only talk to me if no one else is around. And there are some who won't talk to me at all. It's almost as if they're afraid they're going to catch what I have."

Rebecca crossed her arms and thought of those pine trees clinging to the cliffs as the road continued to wind upward. What happened when one walked away from her roots? Roots gave stability, and once she left Montana to go to Oregon, the last of hers would be severed.

She just hoped her fall wouldn't be too hard. Wouldn't hurt too many people.

Would they ever understand that she was really doing it for them?

CHAPTER
4

Rebecca couldn't help but smile when they pulled up to the place Marianna had referred to as a "family cabin." It was a large, two-story home made of logs. They parked in front of a porch, and a small gray dog bounded toward them.

A chuckle slipped from Marianna's lips. "This is Trapper. He used to belong to the former owners of my parents' place, and he adopted me." The dog moved from Marianna to Rebecca and danced around her shoes.

"Hey, Trapper." Rebecca bent down and scratched behind his ear. "Nice to meet you." Then she rose and followed Marianna toward the house. Six natural wood rockers were lined up on the front porch, and Rebecca guessed that they were often filled with family or friends, talking and enjoying the view of the large meadow in front of the house and the mountain range beyond.

Inside the tall door, a gleaming dark wood floor greeted them. There was a small foyer that opened up into a large kitchen and living area. Rebecca took in a breath. Something smelled wonderful. She smiled, remembering how much

Marianna enjoyed baking and cooking—and how much she'd enjoyed it, too, when she'd been with Marianna.

"This would sure be a nice place to have church." The words were out of Rebecca's mouth before she remembered that Marianna was no longer Amish and would no longer have service at her home.

"Well, we do have prayer meetings here. If you'd like to—" She paused and then smiled. "Actually, we can talk about that later. Let's get some lunch first, shall we? Then, after we eat, I can show you to your room."

Marianna sliced pieces of homemade bread and buttered them. Then she moved to an electric cooking pot, took off the lid, and ladled soup into two bowls. "I know I shouldn't say this, but I've fallen in love with my Crock-Pot. I just plug it in and—"

The ringing of Marianna's cell phone interrupted her words, and from the smile on her face when she answered, Rebecca knew it was Ben.

"*Ja*, we made it just fine." Marianna glanced in Rebecca's direction. "She looks great." Laughter spilled out of her. "I'm not sure how long she's staying, but I'll tell her what you said." She pulled the phone from her ear. "Ben said you can stay as long as you'd like. We have plenty of room."

"*Danki*." Rebecca smiled and pulled out a bar stool from the counter and sat.

They chatted for a few minutes, and then Marianna hung up.

"After we eat, would you like to drive back down to the lake with me? Ben's down there swimming with a group of bachelors. They've been playing hard and some of them didn't get lunch."

"Bachelors?"

Marianna placed the soup in front of Rebecca before

turning to a large pantry, opening it, and pulling out a few bags of chips. She then moved to a large cookie jar and began emptying oatmeal cookies into a ziplock bag.

"Sit down, eat. I'll help you with that when you're done." Rebecca fiddled with her spoon. Had Marianna forgotten everything about being Amish?

"*Ach, ja,* I'm sorry." Marianna placed the bag of cookies on the counter and then took her bowl of soup, sitting down beside Rebecca. "We need to pray, don't we?"

Rebecca had lowered her head to pray silently when she felt Marianna's soft, cool hand wrap around hers.

"Dear heavenly Father, first I want to thank you for my friend," Marianna said. "Lord, I thank you that she's been in my life from my first memories. And it means so much that she's come here to be with me—to spend time with me. You know, Lord, how much my heart has ached, thinking of the many friendships I've lost. I don't mind that I've had to face some hardship, because the relationship with You is more beautiful than what I could have imagined. Still, *danki* for my sweet friend's smile. It really lightens my heart. And bless this food. *Ach,* yes, and please keep the guys safe at the lake. I know how bold they can get when they are with each other. I pray You will keep them levelheaded and safe. *Aemen.*"

Marianna's hand released hers. Rebecca blinked, trying to keep the tears at bay as she swallowed down the emotion that built in her throat. Her chest felt warm, and she didn't know why. It was as if Marianna had poured that warm soup right down into her soul.

Rebecca cleared her throat. "*Danki.* I'm glad to be here too." She'd never heard anyone pray like that before. She had heard customers praying out loud at the cafe, but she'd never heard anyone pray as if God was right there in the room with them, sitting on the next bar stool. "I bet it has been hard, guessing what everyone back home is saying."

Marianna shrugged. "It's fine. I know why they say what they say. If the roles were reversed and I was still Amish, I would be saying the same thing—acting the same way."

Rebecca ate her soup, waiting for Marianna to go into more detail. Heaven knows back at home she'd have an earful by now. She'd know who'd said what or who'd treated Marianna with less than a kind attitude. There was very little news that happened in the Amish community back home that didn't bounce from house to house like a ping-pong ball. But Marianna remained silent.

"Would you like more soup? More bread?" she offered.

"Another piece of bread would be great. You are a wonderful baker, Marianna. Ben must be thankful."

"*Ja.*" A chuckle slipped from her lips. She rose and sliced another piece of bread for Rebecca and then hurriedly moved around the kitchen gathering up more snacks for the bachelors. "Ben is very happy with my cooking—especially after being single for so many years—but you should have seen Roy's face when he discovered Ben had packed on a few pounds. Roy is Ben's manager. He's the one who sets up the concerts and such. I wish there was one close that we could go to, but Ben took the month off to enjoy the West Kootenai. In Montana, winter lasts for nine months, and there's just a little slice of summer. You've come at the perfect time."

Rebecca rose and took her bowl to the kitchen sink. Her eyes widened when she saw that Marianna also had a dishwasher, but she decided to say nothing about it. *Why wouldn't she have a dishwasher, not being Amish anymore?*

Rebecca was surprised by how uncomfortable she felt, seeing her friend in an *Englisch* home, hearing her pray out loud . . . And now Rebecca had invaded their vacation time. If it was possible for her to disappear, or slip back outside and find a driver to take her back to the train station, she would. Yet where could she find a driver? She wasn't even sure where the closest neighbor was. And worse than that, what type of wild animal would she meet on the way?

"I'm sorry. I shouldn't have intruded. This is your time together. I could head out tomorrow. I—"

"Nonsense!" The word emerged from Marianna's mouth with force, and she hurried to her friend. She paused before Rebecca, looking into her eyes. "Ben and I have felt led to pray for you. I'm not sure why, but you've been coming to mind a lot lately. When you called, I was so glad to hear from you. I also knew that God had a plan." Marianna offered a soft smile. "This life isn't about just having fun and enjoying ourselves. What good is a beautiful home and cupboards of food if you don't have anyone—have friends—to share it with?" Marianna wrinkled up her nose. "Speaking of which, we better get going. If we don't hurry, those guys might get the idea of catching fish with their bare hands and eating them raw!"

Rebecca laughed and followed her friend to the truck. She didn't understand why Marianna had been thinking of her. She didn't know why she had "just happened" to get Marianna's note right as she left and ended up here, but she was thankful, she supposed. For the past few years—and especially the past few months—she'd felt like God was mad at her. She was hiding so much from her family. She'd been pushing them away. For three years she'd made her plans to leave their community and church, so it was better not to think about God than consider His disapproval. But was it possible that God still thought of her, and that He'd placed her in Marianna's thoughts so she could pray?

Goose bumps rose on Rebecca's arms, and she felt lighter as she climbed into the truck. Lighter than she had for many years. Her chest felt tight and achy, but it wasn't a painful ache. It was a longing for what Marianna had—not the house or the driver's license or even the dishwasher—but the peace, the joy. Rebecca's brow furrowed as she realized that maybe God had a plan in her being here.

Marianna started the truck, but before she put it in gear, she turned in Rebecca's direction.

"You okay?"

Rebecca blew out a breath. "*Ja*. Really I am. Tired, that's all." She rubbed her brow.

"Would you like to stay at the house? To rest?"

"And miss seeing more of Montana? Not to mention those bachelors . . ." Rebecca winked. "Not on your life."

"*Vell*, I'm sure you can't see them swimming. It's really not allowed. The men swim with the men, and the women with the women. But I'll have Ben tell them that you're in town. A few of them are quite handsome. Maybe we should have one or two over for dinner while you're here—"

Rebecca swatted her friend's arm. "Don't you dare. And you know that I wouldn't want to meet them anyway. It was just a joke." She glanced down at her skirt. "Especially not dressed like this."

"Rethinking taking off your Amish clothes, are you?"

Rebecca shrugged. "*Vell*, I haven't really left the Amish, you know. I mean, I left the community . . . but I don't really know where the future is headed."

Marianna turned off the ignition. She turned more fully to face Rebecca.

Rebecca shuffled in her seat, feeling intimidated by her friend's gaze. "Did I say something?"

"No, what you *haven't said* is the problem. You told me that you were coming—that you were on your way. You haven't told me why you left."

Heat radiated through the cab of the truck. Even though the sun was coming through the windshield, even more heat—nervousness—came from within. Rebecca pushed the button to roll down the truck's window. She glanced out at the woods beside Marianna's house, speckled with sunlight and shadow, and then she turned back to Marianna. She swallowed hard. "Aren't the guys hungry? Shouldn't we get going?"

Marianna cocked an eyebrow. "Is the story that long?"

"I suppose not." Rebecca took a deep breath and released it slowly. "The truth is that Montana was just an unexpected stop. I'm on my way to Oregon, where I'm attending nursing school."

"Nursing school? Oregon?" Marianna's brow furrowed. She shook her head as if she hadn't heard Rebecca right. "Nursing school," she mouthed again. Understanding—sympathy—flooded her face.

Rebecca nodded. There was no need to explain. There was no need to mention Claudia's name. How many times had Marianna sat beside her, with an arm around her shoulders, sharing the heartache? Too many times to count.

"I was always afraid to talk to you about . . . about Claudia's death."

"Yeah, most people were," Rebecca said.

"Even as you sat there and cried, *vell*, I didn't know what to say."

"At least you sat with me. It was so strange how people handled things. For weeks after the funeral, people from the community came by. Just to be with us, I suppose. They drove their buggies down the road, entered our house, put jars of canned goods in our cupboards, held baby Claude, and didn't say a word about his mother—about Claudia."

"I'm sorry. I didn't realize . . ."

"Honestly, Marianna, I'm not saying this to make you feel guilty. It was nice seeing that people cared, but it felt fake too. Part of it brought relief because I didn't want them to ask too many questions. I didn't want to try to explain how it happened—especially how I stood there and didn't do a thing to help her. Maybe they were waiting, just waiting for me to tell them . . . but I never did."

Tears rimmed Marianna's eyelids. Trapper barked outside the driver's door, as if knowing something was wrong inside the cab. Marianna's fingers tightened around the steering wheel, but she ignored him. "But . . . how could you have done any different? You didn't know what to do."

"Exactly. Which is why I left Indiana. It's why I'm going to nursing school. I don't want to ever be in that position again. Next time I want to help. I want to be able to save a life, instead of watching it slip away."

Marianna pushed the button to roll down the window and ordered Trapper back to the porch. The dog reluctantly obeyed. Then she reached up and started the truck again, put it in gear, and pulled out onto the dirt road. Birdsong sounded from outside, filtering into the cab of the truck as they drove away.

Marianna glanced over at her, her eyes dark with concern. "And what do your parents think about your decision?"

"They don't know." Rebecca shrugged. "Well, they might now. I left them a letter in my trunk. I didn't have the heart to face them. To see their disappointment."

"And do they know you're with me?"

"*Ne.* I didn't tell them anything. They'd be horrified to

know that I was in West Kootenai, Montana, in an Amish community, with my ex-Amish friend, driving around in a truck with *Englisch* clothes." Rebecca gasped and put a hand over her mouth, trying to make light of it.

"Leaving isn't easy." Marianna swallowed hard. "In fact, the long journey here will probably be the easiest part for you. Leaving is harder than I ever thought . . ."

Rebecca wanted to ask more, but not now. Confessing the truth to her friend was hard enough. Instead Rebecca turned her head, looking out of the truck, and smoothed her hand over her patterned skirt that was just below her knees. It was conservative by the world's standards, but the clothes felt as fancy and revealing as if she'd been wearing cutoff jeans. After all, her calves showed when she walked, and the pattern drew attention to itself—something that Amish dresses never did.

"Just know this." Marianna's voice vibrated as the truck jostled and bounced. "Just know that I'll love you for you—for your heart—and not for your *kapp*."

There was a sadness as Marianna said those words, as if she wished that others—those she'd cared about—had said the same thing to her.

Rebecca wished she had kind words to say to her friend, but maybe just being here was enough. She hoped so. Because as empty and hollow as her soul felt, she had little else to give beyond her presence.

Even though Rebecca couldn't see the bachelors, she could hear them as Marianna parked the truck by the lake.

"See those cliffs over there? There is a nice place to swim right under it. Some guys like to climb up and jump off."

Rebecca gasped. The tallest part of the cliff had to be at least fifty feet tall. "Off of that?"

"*Ach*, no. Not all the way up there." Marianna shook her head. "There are smaller cliffs down below. I've never seen— or heard of—anyone jumping off the top." Marianna pulled out her cell phone and called Ben. "Hey, I'm glad you're still in cell phone range. We're here if you want to come get this food." There was a sweetness in her voice as she said those words.

A few minutes later, Ben made his way to the truck. His hair was damp and hanging in his face, nearly covering his blue eyes. His swimming trunks dripped and his T-shirt clung to him. Rebecca couldn't help but smile. Ben had indeed added a few pounds since the last time she'd seen him back in Shipshewana.

From behind him the voices of the others grew louder as if they were cheering someone on. Rebecca wished she could head to that cliff, just to peek down, but even though Marianna was *Englisch* now, Rebecca knew she'd never allow it.

Rebecca tried to remember if she'd ever known of such a large group of Amishmen from back home who'd taken a day off to swim. She couldn't imagine it happening, even though it was Saturday. If she hadn't been here with Marianna now, she wouldn't have believed it. Back home a *gut* Amishman spent his time working. Occasionally a man took time to fish or to go shooting, but that was frowned upon and brought much embarrassment to his *fraa* if he did it too much.

Ben hurried forward. His feet were shoved into tennis shoes that were untied. The white strings trailed along the dusty ground.

He grinned and extended his hand. "Rebecca, so good to see you!"

She was about to respond when something behind Ben

caught her attention. It was a man—an Amish bachelor, she supposed. He'd climbed to the top of the cliff and was waving to the others down below. His blond hair swooped across his forehead, and he wore only his Amish pants, rolled up to his knees.

Rebecca's heartbeat quickened to see him. He was handsome, and she guessed he was going to follow Ben—and here she was in *Englisch* clothes.

Rebecca shook Ben's hand and then crossed her arms over her chest, wishing she'd brought more Amish clothes since the Amish dress she'd worn onto the train was crumpled and tucked into a corner of her suitcase. She wished she was wearing a neat, pressed Amish dress now. She didn't like the idea of Amish bachelors seeing her dressed in *Englisch* clothes. When she'd left Shipshewana, she'd expected to be leaving all the bachelors behind. Obviously that was not the case. Not that she needed the distraction, but an inner part of her still hoped she could be a wife and mother someday—after she got her degree, of course.

Instead the man barely glanced over his shoulder at them and then moved to the cliff's edge.

She gasped. "He's not going to jump, is he?" Her hand covered her mouth.

Ben turned. "No . . . I don't think so. Caleb's a daredevil, but—"

The words were barely out of Ben's mouth when the handsome bachelor moved toward the cliff and jumped straight out. All three gasped, and Ben rushed to the cliff. If Rebecca hadn't seen it with her own eyes, she wouldn't have believed it.

Yet even before Ben got to the edge, the cheers and laughter coming from the lake calmed the pounding of her heart.

Rebecca looked at Marianna. The color had drained from her cheeks.

"Do things like that always happen around here?" Rebecca placed a hand over her heart. "If so, I'm not sure I can take it."

"I wish I could say this was a onetime thing. I've never seen that"—Marianna pointed to the cliff—"happen before. But with Caleb, there is always something going on."

"Is there at least a clinic nearby for emergencies? Or a doctor? Not that a doctor would be able to help much if he was injured jumping off of that cliff." Worries crowded Rebecca's mind, making the world dim around her. What if something had happened to that bachelor? Was showing off worth risking his life? Making his friends carry the memories if something went wrong?

Ben returned, shaking his head. "That Caleb. I'm not sure what he's going to come up with next."

"Someone should really talk to him." Rebecca crossed her arms. "It's irresponsible."

Ben nodded. "Someone really should, and from the brightness of your cheeks, Rebecca, I can tell it really bothered you. Maybe you should be the one to do it. I've heard that many young women in these parts are fancy on Caleb."

"My cheeks?" She touched her face, and it indeed felt hot, but she was certain it was just from the warmth of the sun. "I'd talk to him if I felt I had any right. But I . . ." Her words twisted around her tongue, and she wasn't sure how to finish the sentence. "I have no intentions of being fancy on anyone, honestly I don't."

Ben and Marianna cast sideways glances at each other, and she could tell they were amused. Did they think she'd been attracted to his antics? Not even close. Well, at least not completely. She was just worried about Caleb. Yes, that was it. Worried about anyone who didn't take danger seriously, who didn't realize how one event—one day—could change everything.

The sun beamed on Caleb's shoulders as he took a big bite of his sandwich. "Ben, did you say Marianna had a sister? I need a *fraa* who's not only willing to feed me, but also all my friends." He chuckled.

Ben brushed his hair back from his face, and it was impossible to hide his smile. "I found someone special, all right, in Marianna. But I'm sorry to say her next oldest sister just started school."

Caleb put the sandwich down on the towel he was sitting on and began to cough. "Fifteen years, *ja*. I can wait."

"*Voll schpaas.*" Ben chuckled. "Very funny."

Caleb cocked his eyebrow. "*Voll schpaas, ja?* You're speaking Pennsylvania Dutch now? Not bad for a popular singer from Los Angeles."

Ben shrugged. Then he pulled out the zippered bag of cookies and passed them around. "Marianna isn't the only one who's made changes after our marriage. She's had to speed up her life a little, and I've had to slow mine down. She's learned about dishwashers and driving a car, and I've learned to tell her mem that her meals are *appenditlich*."

"*Ja.*" Amos pointed to Ben's stomach, which pooched out a little under his wet T-shirt. "I can tell you've been practicing that one plenty yet."

Ben smiled and took another bite of cookie. "A man's got to do what a man's got to do."

Caleb stretched out his legs in the sun, thankful for food he didn't have to prepare or buy. Since tomorrow wasn't a church Sunday, he had to pick up some items at the store tonight. They also had to get items for their big wagon trip on Tuesday.

"Ben, did Marianna happen to get that shopping list for us, for our wagon trip? I should get everything tonight. I don't want to be caught by any church members filling up a shopping cart on Sunday—even if it's an off week."

Ben lowered his gaze, as if intent on the lettuce peeking out from his sandwich. "Actually, I have some news about that: I don't think Marianna and I are going."

"What?" Caleb's jaw dropped. "But it was your and Ike's idea."

"I know, but there've been a few changes. Mari has a friend in town—from back in Indiana."

"Is she pretty?" Amos' eyes brightened. "You should invite her."

"Uh, I'm not sure Rebecca would be interested in a wagon ride." Ben cleared his throat. "But it's more than that. Marianna doesn't want anyone to know . . . but she's expecting a baby."

Caleb reached over and patted his shoulder. "That's wonderful news!" Yet when he looked closer at Ben's face, he could see there was a problem.

"It is good news, yes, but we've only been married a year and we've had some losses already . . ." Ben stopped there, and Caleb wasn't going to prod.

Caleb felt sad for his friend. One of his sisters had faced the same type of struggles, and he'd seen her many tears. Yet even as he felt his mood darken, he pushed the thoughts away. It was better not to think of that loss. Of any loss. Instead he turned his mind back to the food.

"And who'll be doing the cooking? Ike?" Caleb winced.

"You'd think an older bachelor like that would have learned to cook at least a little to be able to survive living on his own all these years. I guess that's why he's so friendly—in order to get a lot of dinner invitations."

Ben stroked his jaw. "Actually, we've got that covered. Both Annie Johnson from the store and Millie Arnold have offered to come along and cook."

Laughter burst from Amos. "Well, Caleb, you were hoping for some ladies to come along."

Caleb frowned. A middle-aged store owner and an elderly widow weren't his idea of fun company. He turned to Ben. "So . . . tell me a little more about Marianna's friend. She wouldn't want to ride along, would she? I love Millie, but I'd rather share a seat on the wagon with someone who's not my grandmother's age."

"*Vell*, Rebecca . . . she's not a typical Amish woman. Marianna loves her dearly, but I've heard stories. Even though Rebecca was Marianna's closest friend, Marianna said she began to wander as they got older. She smoked cigarettes and didn't attend church often. It saddened Mari that Rebecca worked at an *Englisch* bakery and often spent the weekend with her *Englisch* friends. Marianna didn't even want to consider what Rebecca was up to during those long weekends."

"Maybe she's changing." Amos' voice seemed hopeful. "Maybe she's come to try to make things right."

"*Vell*, she wouldn't do that by coming to stay with her friend who just recently left the Amish." Ben sighed. "She showed up today with just a day's notice—headed off cross-country alone. I'm not sure where she's headed next, but she's not going to be one you find sitting in front of a fire on a cold winter's night, working on her quilt frame . . ."

Ben continued, turning his attention to the menu that

Annie and Millie had already planned, but Caleb's mind hadn't followed his words. Instead he thought of Marianna's friend. Even though Ben's words had been meant to discourage him, they did just the opposite. Especially the part about Rebecca heading off across the country alone. It sounded adventurous, brave. It seemed Rebecca would be someone Caleb would like to get to know.

CHAPTER

5

Rebecca couldn't help but watch in the side mirror of the truck as Marianna drove away—just in case the bachelor climbed up that cliff and attempted it again. Not that she wanted him to try it. One wrong twist of his body, and he could seriously injure himself. In EMT class she'd read all the horror stories of such feats.

"Do you mind if we stop by my friend Susan's house before we head home?" Marianna interrupted her thoughts. "I need to return her sewing machine. I used it to sew a few new doll dresses for Ellie's birthday."

Rebecca cocked an eyebrow. "An electric sewing machine?"

"*Ja*, and I have to say it is faster. And there was even an attachment that allowed me to make tiny little buttonholes with just one push."

Rebecca gasped, feigning shock. "Buttons?"

Marianna shook her head. "It's a doll dress, *ja*. It's not like Mem would allow anyone in her home to wear a garment with buttons."

Rebecca wanted to tease Marianna more, but she could tell that it bothered her. Marianna no doubt felt the condemnation

of enough people that she didn't need Rebecca jumping in—
even if she was only joking.

Halfway back from the lake, they drove by a simple log
home. Marianna pointed. "That's where Mem and Dat live.
They're renting for now, and it's a little small—especially now
that the kids are getting older—but there's this beautiful pond
a bit out back, and they have the best neighbors."

Marianna didn't say anything about taking Rebecca to see
them. Why? Rebecca had spent as much time at their house as
her own during her growing-up years. She'd slept over many
nights, and she and Marianna had often stayed up late dreaming of their future husbands and children. Rebecca folded her
hands on her lap. Tension tightened in her chest.

They never would have imagined this—now. Marianna
wearing plain clothes and a head covering, driving an automo-
bile. And Rebecca in *Englisch* clothes, questioning when she'd
ever return to their small community in Indiana. Her heart
ached, and she missed the innocence of that time.

They pulled up to a large ranch, and Marianna parked the
truck. There was a corral with a horse and fields that stretched
out, ending in a dense forest of pine trees. An American flag
waved in the wind, and the sign over the door read *Carash*.
Rebecca held her breath, almost expecting a man to exit wearing a cowboy hat. Marianna unloaded the sewing machine from
the cab and carried it to the door with Rebecca behind her.

Less than thirty seconds later, it was a woman who exited
wearing western jeans and a pink flannel shirt. "Marianna?
Girl, get in here. Is this your friend you were talking about?"

"Yes, Susan. Can you believe Rebecca came all this way to
see me?" She handed over the sewing machine, but Susan gave
it little attention. She placed the machine on the side table and
then motioned them in.

"Of course she came all the way to see you. I can believe that." Susan chuckled. "With a friend like you it's worth every mile." She waved both of them closer.

Rebecca immediately felt comfortable with Marianna's friend. "You have a beautiful place here."

"Thanks, it belonged to Dave's parents. It's a lot of work—caring for the cows, the horses. We lost our barn a few years ago, but thankfully the good people in this community helped us to raise a new one."

"Really? That's wonderful." Rebecca had heard of the Amish having barn raisings for each other, but she'd never heard of it being done for an *Englisch* person. Maybe this place was different.

"Come on in, and don't worry about kicking off your shoes at the door. I haven't swept in two days, and any dirt that you bring in isn't going to do a lick of harm." Susan laughed as they entered and shook her head. "I was a city girl, you know." She kicked off one of her boots. "If you would have told me I'd be living here, taking care of cows and horses and chickens, I wouldn't have believed you." She pulled off the other boot.

"Susan . . . I've never heard that before. That you were a city girl."

Susan motioned to the kitchen table. Marianna and Rebecca sat, and without even asking if they were thirsty, Susan poured three large glasses of lemonade from a pitcher from the fridge.

"Oh yes, I can't believe I haven't told you. My father used to manage a hotel in downtown Chicago. I met Dave when some friends and I took one summer to visit as many national parks as we could, including Glacier National Park, which is right up the road. We got twenty parks under our belt, but there was only one guy who stood out. When Dave invited me back here to meet his parents, I had no idea where he was taking me. Or what I was in for. They were old-time ranchers through and through."

"Did they accept you?" Rebecca took a sip of her lemonade, forgetting for a time that Susan was *Englisch* and so different from anyone she'd ever met.

"I had to play it tough," Susan continued. "When Dave brought me home, the first thing out of his mother's mouth was, 'You didn't bring home a princess, did you?' I had no idea how to muck a stall or butcher a chicken, but that didn't hinder me. I'm convinced that we can achieve more than we ever thought possible and succeed where others expect us to fail . . . if we just put our minds to it." Susan barely took a breath and then turned to Rebecca, offering a warm smile. "Speaking of which, Marianna told me her Amish friend was coming, but you look as *Englisch* as my daughter. Is this the first stop in some grand adventure?"

"Yes, actually. I'm on my way to nursing school. Over the last few years I took Emergency Medical Technician classes and started college classes too." Rebecca glanced at Marianna out of the corner of her eye, waiting for her response.

Marianna paused with her glass to her mouth, as if she wasn't sure she'd heard that right. "Like . . . real college?"

Rebecca looked at her friend. "*Ja*, like real college."

"But how is that possible? You don't have your high school diploma."

Rebecca smiled. "Actually, I do. I have all my high school credits and an Associate of Science in Nursing too."

"But when? How? I only left one and a half years ago. Surely you couldn't have done all that during that time."

"I've been taking online classes for three years. Pam at the Shipshewana library has been helping me. I've only been working half time—less than half time actually. Pam lives one street over from the bakery. I'd cut through the alley and do my work on her computer."

"I—I don't understand. Why didn't you tell me?"

"You were the perfect Amish woman, Marianna. You did everything right. I knew for certain you'd try to make me change my mind. Either that or you'd somehow let it slip, and before long my parents would know."

Marianna's fingers drummed on the table, and her jaw dropped in disbelief. "And all those weekends you went to the next community over to visit your *rumspringa* friends? What about that?"

"There were no other friends. I stayed with Pam, and she helped me with my papers and tests. Well, except for the weekends when I was taking an EMT class. Then I was in Elkhart with some people who opened their home to me."

A chair leg scraped on the wooden floor, and Rebecca remembered again that they weren't alone. When she glanced over at Susan Carash, a large grin parted the woman's lips. "I am so proud of you!" Susan hurried to the cupboard and pulled out a large chocolate bar. "I've been saving this for a special occasion. More than once I had to tell my kids to keep their mitts off of it . . . I just love it when someone discovers who they are and decides to follow their dreams."

Rebecca nodded and smiled, not knowing what else to say.

Marianna didn't look as convinced. Her lips pressed into a tight line. "So, what did your parents say about that?"

Rebecca took a sip of lemonade and shrugged. "They don't know. Like I told you earlier, they have no idea where I went. I kept the letter to them as simple as possible. As far as they know, I've left the Amish . . . and I didn't have the heart to tell them why."

The two other women sat silently, looking at each other as if wondering what to say to Rebecca.

Finally, Susan stood and moved to the fridge. "This seems like a time to shell peas, if you ask me."

Rebecca cocked her head and chuckled at the woman's comment. "Shell peas?"

Susan grabbed a large strainer filled with pea pods and placed it in the center of the table. Then she offered each of them a paper towel for the pods and a plastic bowl for the peas.

She seemed eager as they sat down, and her gaze turned back to Rebecca. "I'm sorry, I didn't mean to interrupt you, but my mother-in-law always said the words flow better when one's hands are busy," she said.

Sitting around the table shelling peas reminded Rebecca of the sewing circles she'd grown up going to. It was a time when Amish women came together, and as their hands worked, their stories were shared freely.

Marianna shelled a few peas and then paused and turned to her friend. "Have you been thinking about this long—thinking about leaving?" she dared to ask. The grayish color of her eyes reminded Rebecca of smoke rising from a fire. Only this time, instead of reflecting the happiness Rebecca usually saw in her friend's gaze, they reflected sadness, betrayal.

Rebecca readjusted herself in the wooden chair. Her body ached after the long train ride. More than that, her heart ached for the betrayal Marianna felt.

"When my sister died, I felt helpless. I can't save the world. I know that. People will get hurt. People will die, even in a community like ours. But I want to know that if I'm ever in that situation again, I can do something to help."

"I understand that, Rebecca, but how is that possible? Do

you really think our community will welcome you home after you finish your schooling?"

"Maybe not ours . . . and maybe not another Amish community. At least I don't think they'll just open their homes to me. But . . . what if I can be an educator? I can teach the midwives, who can teach the women. Maybe they will learn to trust me. Maybe they'll let me into their lives . . . eventually."

From the look on Marianna's face, she didn't think the idea would work. Rebecca didn't want to argue.

"My friend Lora is part of the Mennonite community around Goshen," Rebecca continued. "If I lived there, it's close enough to hear what's happening in my family's life without shaming them by being too close. A lot of people I know who used to be Amish are involved in the Mennonite church there. Maybe I can start educating *them*."

"All of us need to be better educated." It was Susan who'd piped up this time. Her paper towel had double the amount of empty shells that Rebecca's or Marianna's had. Then again, Susan's mind was on only one thing. Susan chuckled. "It's not that we ever get too much learning, and it seems that as we plan to teach others, God often makes us the pupil first, just so we get the lesson real deep within before we try to share it."

Marianna sighed. "And then, even when we think we've learned the lesson, God reminds us that we're just first-grade students in this thing called *life*." She reached over and patted Rebecca's hand. "I'm worried about you leaving everything like that. Maybe because I know how hard it's been for me, and even how hard it's been for Ben." Marianna's voice trembled. "One moment I know I've made the right decision, and five minutes later I question myself on why I did what I did. And with you . . . it's not too late. You can get back on that train. You can return to that life. Things can be the same."

Susan didn't say anything then. How could an *Englischer* ever understand? She couldn't, and Susan must have realized that when she rose and mumbled something about forgetting to check the mail before hurrying out the front door.

"I hear what you're saying." Rebecca reached out and took Marianna's hand, squeezing it tight. "I'm giving up my family, my community, and most likely finding love . . . But if someone else—even one person—won't have to face the same loss, then it's worth it." She released Marianna's hand and instead placed it over her own heart. "And even though I'm leaving a lot, I'm not leaving God. If one *gut* thing came out of growing up Amish and hearing about His goodness, I know that."

CHAPTER

6

On the drive home, Marianna hummed along to Ben's CD playing in the CD player. Rebecca waited for Marianna to pelt her with more questions. Didn't she want to know when Rebecca planned on leaving Montana, when classes started in Portland, or where she'd live in Oregon? Rebecca expected her to ask about nursing school and how Rebecca had managed to hide her online classes from everyone. She even expected Marianna to get mad—to confront her about her lies through the years. But it didn't happen. Instead Marianna talked about her mem's garden, where she had her own plot.

"Our house wasn't finished when it was time to plant, so I just added a few extra rows at Mem's place. This is the first time my parents put in a large garden in Montana—now that they know they're staying."

Rebecca wanted to ask what had changed their minds. Why had they decided to stay? Like Rebecca, they'd faced losses back in Indiana—the loss of two daughters. Maybe, like her, they were running from the memories. But unlike them, Rebecca wasn't looking for a new place. She was looking for a life that could help others live better. Help save people from heartache.

When they got back to the house, Marianna showed Rebecca around. The place had four bedrooms and three baths; a modern, indoor laundry room; and a full basement that Ben had turned into a recording studio.

They moved back upstairs, heading to the extra bedrooms.

Marianna paused by the doorway of the small room next to the master bedroom. Except for one simple dresser it was empty. Did Marianna hope to someday fill it with baby things?

"This is not how I planned my life," Marianna finally said. "I'm not only learning about being married, but also about not following the Amish ways. I'm thankful for the foundation of community and faith that I was raised with, but I'm learning to trust in Jesus more—trust that what He's done is more than what I could ever do."

"*Ja,* of course." There was an awkward silence. "Do you mind if I unpack?" Rebecca asked.

"*Ne,* of course I don't mind."

Rebecca made her way back to the cozy room where she was staying. The centerpiece of the space was a log bed with a colorful handmade quilt. There was also a trunk, a rag rug, and white curtains in the window. The only thing that differed from a typical Amish bedroom was a few prints of wild roses hanging on one wall.

Marianna had set her friend's suitcase inside the door, and Rebecca carried it to the bed, opening it. Had her parents found the note she'd left them? What did they think? She'd told them not to worry, but she had a feeling they would.

Rebecca pulled out four pairs of jeans and two skirts from her suitcase and placed them on the bed. She also pulled out her *kapp* that she'd taken off on the train.

"I thought you gave that up." Her best friend's voice caused her to jump.

Rebecca fingered her *kapp*. "*Vell*, I still haven't decided if I'm staying Amish. I mean, I haven't turned my back on it completely."

"I'm not talking about that." Marianna clicked her tongue and pointed to the cigarettes Rebecca had hidden under her blouses. "In the last letter you said you gave up your habit."

"*Ach*, those." Rebecca picked up the pack and carried it to the trash by the small desk, tossing it in. "I found them in my dresser drawer when I was packing—didn't remember they were there. I knew Mem would be looking through my things and . . . I didn't want her to find them."

Rebecca bit her lip. All that was true, but a truth she wasn't going to share was that she'd also kept them in case she needed a smoke. Not that she smoked often—but during tense moments it calmed her. Even being here with her friend, in this beautiful room, made her feel as if her head was in a vice. Maybe she just needed to break free completely and head to Portland like she'd planned.

Instead she blew out a big breath and met Marianna in the kitchen, watching her cook. A frown marred Marianna's face as she cut up vegetables. Gone was the smile that had been there most of the day. It was Rebecca's news that had robbed it away.

Rebecca looked around. Her heart pinched at the small dining room table and the Bible that sat in the middle of it. There was a print on the wall with wedding vows and one photo of Ben and Marianna's wedding. Ben had built this home for her, and to watch the way he looked at her was something Rebecca envied. Something she didn't know if she'd ever find. Especially now. She was walking away from the Amish community and stepping into a world that frightened her. Marianna had found a man who loved God and who worked to understand her and what growing up Amish had meant to her. Would there ever be someone like that for Rebecca?

Marianna made a delightful dinner of rib eye steaks and mashed potatoes, followed by soft, chewy peanut butter cookies. Ben exclaimed after each bite as if it was the best meal he'd ever had.

After they loaded the dishwasher—which Rebecca had to admit would be easy to get used to—they moved out to the chairs on the porch. As they rocked, Rebecca sat with her nerves on edge, waiting for Marianna to say something more about college. Instead her oldest friend just stared into the meadow with a soft smile on her lips. She was more peaceful than she had been before, and Rebecca knew that had everything to do with Ben.

The air had cooled, but it was still warm enough to enjoy the evening without a sweater. Tall mountains rose over the forest of trees. The air was filled with the scent of pine and the lilac bush planted near the porch steps.

Marianna sat in the chair next to her husband. Ben's hair was tousled and uncombed after a shower. He strummed his guitar to a simple tune. Were there words to that song that ran through his head? If so, it was something romantic. Rebecca could see it from the way he glanced at Marianna every so often. She could see it in the way heat rose to Marianna's cheeks. The mood was intimate and lazy. Marianna sipped on a cup of iced tea. Rebecca had tea, too, but her mind couldn't relax enough to enjoy it.

Why hadn't Marianna said *anything* about her schooling to come? Over dinner they'd chatted about friends and life back in Indiana, and a few times it seemed as if Marianna was going to divert to a more serious topic, but then she'd pause and press her lips together. What kept Marianna from asking more? Didn't she care? Wasn't she worried?

"Rebecca?"

"*Ja?*"

"I was thinking of heading to the store. There's going to be a church potluck tomorrow, and I realized I'm out of a few things."

"A potluck?" Rebecca scratched her temple.

"*Ach*, it's like the lunches we usually had after the Amish church, except the people at the community church we attend now are a little more elaborate. Instead of sandwiches with peanut butter and spread, they bring things like green bean casserole, chocolate cake, and fried chicken."

"It sounds *appenditlich*. But . . . you don't mind if I attend the Amish church here, do you?"

"No—uh—of course not. But tomorrow is the off week. You're welcome to stay home, of course, or . . . you could visit our community church."

Rebecca rocked in the chair, wondering how to answer that. She was disappointed. Deep down she'd been a little hopeful of seeing that handsome bachelor again. But visiting Marianna's church seemed better than staying here alone.

"*Vell*, maybe I will go with you . . . just once, to see. After all, you did say they have fried chicken."

Ben and Marianna chuckled, looking pleased with her decision.

Rebecca cleared her throat. "But I'm embarrassed about the next question: do you have an Amish dress I can borrow? I only have the one I wore to get on the train, and it's not washed. I had no plans to wear my Amish clothes in my nursing classes, but now that I'm here . . . well . . ."

"I understand. It's hard not to dress Amish in an Amish community. Would you like to borrow one now to go to the store too?"

Rebecca felt a heaviness lift at her friend's words. Maybe Marianna understood better than she thought.

"If you don't mind . . ."

"Not at all."

Ten minutes later Rebecca was clothed in Marianna's Amish dress and apron and her own *kapp*. She never thought she'd feel this way, but she felt more herself in those Amish clothes than she had in a long time.

Rebecca got into the truck first. Ben gave Marianna a quick kiss on the cheek as she climbed into the driver's seat.

"Pick me up something yummy from the store." Ben winked at his wife.

Marianna chuckled. "The peanut butter cookies weren't enough dessert?"

Ben shook his head. "Now, dear, you know that my dessert stomach is twice as big as my dinner stomach."

"*Ja*, all right, but you have to be the one to tell Roy that you're not sticking to the diet he put you on."

Ben shrugged. "Well, that may be true, but just think of all my exercise. It was a lot of work climbing up those cliffs and jumping."

Marianna's eyes grew wide. "You didn't climb up to the top and jump, did you?" Rebecca saw fear in her friend's gaze.

"Nah, I'll leave those feats to Caleb. Speaking of which . . ." Ben leaned farther into the truck cab and looked Rebecca's direction. "I told Caleb about you. The other bachelors too— but Caleb was immediately intrigued. He said he thought it was gutsy that an Amish woman would travel by herself on the train from Indiana to Montana."

"*Ja, vell* . . . I'm not sure how impressive running away is."

Marianna offered a sympathetic look. "You're not just running to leave. You're running to be trained, to help people, right?"

Rebecca nodded, glad that Marianna at least understood that much.

It only took them a couple minutes to drive to the store. As the truck neared, Rebecca saw a handful of bachelors entering.

"Heading there for dinner, I suppose," Marianna said offhandedly.

Five bachelors walked in a line across the gravel parking lot, and Rebecca immediately recognized Caleb. He was a few inches taller than the others and had a thin but muscular build. Instead of an Amish shirt, he wore a red T-shirt with his Amish pants and big work boots that seemed inappropriate for such a nice summer evening. The other bachelors gave Marianna's truck no mind as it drove and parked, but Caleb watched them over his shoulder, eyeing the truck and especially the passenger.

Rebecca swallowed hard and fiddled with the string of her *kapp*. His eyes met hers, and she looked to her lap. With wide strokes she brushed her fingers across her white apron, as if she were brushing away crumbs. She refused to look, but she could feel his gaze. Only when Marianna pulled the keys from the ignition and climbed from the truck did Rebecca dare to look up from her lap.

"I think I'll stay here, if you don't mind."

"What? Didn't you see the bachelors go in? I wanted to introduce you around."

Rebecca released a sigh. "You know it'll just make things harder. If I make friends, well . . . I'm not going to be here long."

Marianna blinked slowly. Her gray eyes focused on Rebecca. "*Ja*, all right, then. I'll only be a few minutes. Unless Millie Arnold is in here. She's a sweet lady, but when one runs into her, one has to expect at least a ten-minute conversation just to hear the updates on everyone and everything."

Rebecca nodded. "I'm fine."

She watched as Marianna entered, and through the glass door and window could see her talking to the clerk behind the front counter. The store was made of logs and had a wide porch that was cluttered with an ice machine, propane tanks, and a few benches. The minutes passed, and she questioned if she was being a fool. She could be—should be—friendly.

Rebecca thought about the handsome bachelor with his curious gaze. He was a daredevil—wasn't that what Ben had said? That was the last thing she needed—a man. Especially now, with her studies. She also didn't need to be attracted to someone who didn't realize the seriousness of his actions. One wrong move and Caleb could hurt himself or someone else.

More minutes passed, and Rebecca picked up Ben's CD case from the center console. She grinned, looking at the picture of him. In real life he was handsome, but the cover of the CD made him look as though he could be a model for some fancy magazine. As she set it down, a knocking on her side window startled her. She jumped and glanced up to see Caleb with a wide-eyed gaze.

"Rebecca?" she heard him say through the window glass.

"*Ja?*"

He motioned for her to roll down the window. She looked at the door for a handle to roll it down. There wasn't a handle, but there was a small lever. She pushed against it but nothing happened. Maybe it didn't work if the truck wasn't running.

Rebecca motioned for Caleb to step back, and then she opened the door and stepped out.

Caleb looked at her without a hint of a smile. "Marianna sent me out with a message. She has a big order she's picking up, and she wants to know if you'll turn the truck around for her so she can load everything up in the back easier."

Rebecca tilted her head slightly, wondering if he was joking. The bachelor crossed his arms over his chest and didn't seem to be. He didn't crack a smile. She imagined he'd be even handsomer if he did—if that was possible.

"But the keys . . ."

He glanced in the cab of the truck, and she followed his gaze. "Uh, *ja*, Marianna said they'd be in the ignition."

"And . . . she wants me to turn it around?" Rebecca touched her *kapp*. "I don't think those in the Amish community would approve of that."

"*Ach*, you didn't hear?"

"Hear what?"

"In this community things are a bit different. It's all right to drive a car—or a truck—if it's less than one hundred yards' distance. There's all types of emergencies, like carrying a new calf to the barn, moving a load of logs from the wooded area behind one's house to the woodpile, or in this case an extra-large grocery order."

"But I'm Amish . . . Why would you think I know how to drive?"

Caleb leaned in closer and eyed her. His blue eyes sparkled, causing butterflies to dance in her gut. "Are you saying you don't know how?"

She tilted up her chin and met the challenge in his gaze. "Well, my friend Pam—the librarian—did give me a few driving lessons. She told me that I might want to consider—"

Rebecca pinched her lips together. She couldn't believe she'd nearly told Caleb about leaving the Amish and about school. She hadn't minded talking to Susan, Ben, and Marianna about it. She trusted that they'd all keep her plans to themselves. But within the Amish community things were different. A lot of sharing went on. If she didn't watch her words, news could get back and her parents would be on the next train.

"Never mind how I know. I suppose I'll try."

With a touch at the back of his hat brim, the bachelor tilted it forward, but Rebecca still caught a glimpse of the humor in his gaze. He watched as she walked around the truck to the driver's seat. She couldn't help but see the admiration in his eyes as she climbed in, shut the door, started the truck, and put it in reverse. She pressed gently on the gas and backed the truck onto the gravel road, drove up a little, and then turned the truck around and parked it so that the back end was by the store's front door.

His laughter met her ears as she turned off the engine and climbed out.

"You did it! And a good job too. It was just a little jerky, but nothing that wouldn't smooth out with practice."

She hopped down from the truck and walked around to him. "Well, I suppose I'm glad you approve. Now . . . do you think Marianna might need a hand with all those groceries? A good Amishman would offer, you know."

"*Ja*, of course."

Caleb moved to the store but paused at the door, opening it just as Marianna stepped out. In one hand she carried a small ziplock bag with some type of white powder. In the other was a foil tin of cinnamon rolls. Marianna took two steps to the truck and then paused.

"Did someone move my truck?"

"*Ja.*" Rebecca stepped forward. "Do you need help with your things?"

"This?" Marianna held up the bag. "This is all I have. I was out of baking soda. I borrowed some from Annie. I'm sorry it took me so long. Annie got started telling me about their upcoming wagon-train vacation, and I finally had to butt in and tell her you were waiting. Is that what you thought—that I'd have a lot? Is that why you turned the truck around?"

Rebecca blinked slowly and then turned to Caleb, who had a blank look on his face. She expected him to answer, but instead laughter poured from his lips. "I cannot believe that— that you fell for that." His voice was winded from his chuckling.

Marianna's laughter met Rebecca's ears next, and Rebecca turned to her friend, shocked.

"You think it's funny too? What if your truck had gotten damaged? You shouldn't just leave the keys in it—you never know who could be around. And more than that"— she turned to Caleb and pointed a finger his direction—"you should be ashamed of lying!"

He shrugged. "I should be." Then he offered her a grin.

Marianna laughed even harder.

Rebecca resisted the urge to stomp off. She wanted to, but she hadn't been paying good enough attention. She didn't know which dirt road would take her back to Marianna's house. "Please, can we just go? And what's so funny?"

Marianna carried her ziplock bag and cinnamon rolls to the driver's seat with a lightness in her step. "I never thought I'd see the day when someone would give you a run for your money, that's all." She seemed more open than she had earlier. More like the old Marianna. "Why, Rebecca. I think you've met your match!"

Two other bachelors emerged from the store, and it was

clear they'd been watching from inside. Neither of them seemed amused. One of the shorter guys approached Caleb and playfully knocked the side of his head. "You better be careful who you encourage to do what. This truck could have ended up running through that window and over Edgar's cash register."

"Oh no." Rebecca straightened her shoulders. "I've learned to watch out for *Englisch*men, so it's Caleb who was risking his life. If I would have run over anyone . . . it would have been him," she huffed.

Caleb's eyes brightened as she said his name, and he smiled.

"Speaking of Edgar, Annie just told me there's a surprise party for him tomorrow night at my parents' place," Marianna said.

"But I thought that was next week," one of the bachelors said.

"Annie's coming with us now, don't you remember, Amos?" This time it was Caleb who playfully shoved his friend. "I suppose she pushed it up."

"*Ja*." Marianna nodded. "And I'm sorry we can't make it with all of you on the wagon vacation. It sounds like those logging roads could have been quite the adventure . . ." Marianna softly bit her lower lip and looked away.

"Did you have plans?" Rebecca felt her heart sink. "I shouldn't have just showed up like this. I should have just gone on to—" Rebecca halted her words, noticing the eyes of the bachelors upon her.

"We did have plans, but we backed out even before we knew you were coming." Marianna touched Rebecca's hand. "You weren't the reason, I promise." Marianna swallowed and then turned her attention toward the bachelors. "Caleb, Amos, and a few others are going to Libby and back on old logging roads. Ben and I talked about it. It's just not a good time for us.

I mean, he just finished filming his video yesterday. It's been so busy . . ." Yet even as Marianna said those words, Rebecca could see it was more than that. She'd known Marianna enough years to know that when her eyebrows pushed together and the skin folded on her forehead, something was wrong. She also saw from Marianna's tight-lipped gaze that she wasn't going to change her mind.

"But as for the surprise party?" Caleb interjected again. He directed the question to Marianna, but his eyes moved toward Rebecca, hopeful, and then back again.

Marianna smiled. "If Rebecca doesn't mind, I would like to go."

"*Ja*. We can do that. Sunday evenings are always a *gut* time to spend with friends." The words shot out before she had a chance to stop them.

Caleb's eyebrows lifted slightly. His eyes widened with excitement.

"I mean, it would be good to meet everyone, wouldn't it?" Rebecca touched the back edge of her *kapp*. "After all, Marianna has said such wonderful things about her neighbors . . ."

She forced herself not to look at Caleb. She told herself it was the fresh mountain air that had her heart pumping so. She had nursing school waiting. She had *Englisch* clothes back at Marianna's house. She hadn't even been planning to wear these Amish clothes, yet here she was. Even if Caleb did find interest in her, he would soon be disappointed. As much as her interest was piqued by this handsome bachelor, he could be no more than a friend. Good thing he was leaving for that wagon ride. Good thing that tomorrow night would be the only time she'd spend with him. Tuesday morning he'd be heading out on his own adventure, leaving her mind and heart to focus on her journey to come.

CHAPTER

7

Caleb rolled over on his bunk, wishing he could train his body not to stir so early. There were no cows to milk, no team to hitch up to the plow, but all those years of waking up on the farm had done the trick.

The room had just started to lighten from the morning's first rays, and his thoughts went to Marianna Stone's pretty friend. There was no denying he found Rebecca interesting. Even though she looked similar to any typical Amish girl, her confidence intrigued him. She'd come all this way from Indiana alone, and something told him she was used to going solo.

Caleb jumped up, dressed in his clothes he'd tossed on the floor before bed, then ran his fingers through his hair. It was still early yet—too early to stoke the fire and get the coffee-pot going. Amos had complained more than once that if he'd wanted someone banging around in the morning, he would have stayed back in Ohio at his mem's house.

Opening the curtains wider, he watched as the first rays of dawn lit the eastern sky, and he marveled at the color of pink that tinted the horizon. It was the same color that had tinted

Rebecca's cheeks as she'd forced herself not to look at him. Leave it to his luck that the only girl he wanted paying attention to him was the one who forced herself to look away.

Caleb changed his socks and slid them into his mud-caked boots, thankful that it was an off Sunday. It wasn't that he didn't like church. He didn't like the pressure. He didn't like the looks that he received from the mothers of the eligible young women in town. He even didn't like that more than one single woman would bring him a large slice of pie that she'd made just for him. The pie was good, but the expectations in their eyes made him nervous.

Usually he'd head out to visit neighbors or go fishing, but this morning he'd spend a little time packing for the trip. He tried not to be disappointed that Annie and Millie were coming instead of Ben and Marianna. At least he would have some good food. He wished he could ask Rebecca to go. He liked her. Liked her spunk.

Even now he smiled, remembering how she'd fallen for his joke and turned the truck around. He couldn't think of another Amish woman who would have done that.

Caleb picked up a few pairs of pants from the floor and smelled them. These were the ones he hadn't worn to work, and they didn't smell too dirty. He took them over to the knapsack he borrowed, folding them to put inside, when he noticed something was already there. It was the stack of letters from the counter. He took them out and tossed them on his bed.

"You need to read them, Caleb. You can't run from home forever," Amos mumbled.

So much for not waking his friend.

"I'm not running. It's just that I don't need to read what's happening. I can guess."

"It's your family, Caleb. They care for you. They want to know you care back."

"I care. I send them postcards."

"*Ja*, that will make everything right again, won't it?"

Caleb looked at the pile of letters. They were still stacked as they'd come in. Fear gripped his chest as he looked at the one that had come in just a few days ago. No, he didn't want to read that one. Didn't want to hear how bad off things had gotten. Instead he took the letter from the bottom of the stack—the oldest one from three months prior—and opened it.

Dear Caleb,

I can't believe you've been gone three months already. The first shoots are already peeking in the fields. Your sisters came by yesterday—and some of our neighbors—and helped me clean for church. It feels gut to have it done. Miriam was even on her knees scrubbing the floorboards. She's always been the one to fret over all the details.

We've come to know the neighbors down the street yet. Joe and Mattie Beiler are building a home on his grandfather's property. I've been taking them a bit of leftovers, which helps them. They are living in the basement as they build the house on top and she appreciates anything I bring. The truth is, without you and Opa eating, I cook too much. I'm just used to it, I suppose. Those two empty chairs at the table should remind me, but someone my age is set in her ways.

Things are the same. Not much to report healthwise. It makes me think that we should all be more thankful for our days and the quality of our years.

I hope you will write and tell us some about Montana. We read in the Budget that folks haven't planted their gardens in the ground yet. I suppose that makes sense, being so high in the mountains and all. It's good for those who have a greenhouse and get an early start.

Your dat seems more tired than normal, but that's to be expected. There are those who come and help, but it's not the same as before. Daily chores do take us so much time.

Have you thought, yet, about coming home just for a week for Miriam and Will's wedding? Maybe they'd even want you to be a nava hucker if they knew you were coming back. The wedding was just published, and although a spring wedding isn't common here, it's more common where Will is from.

Please write, son, and let us know how you are. It's hard enough not having a father to talk to. Having a son gone is harder yet, but I suppose there is just a short window when a man can have such adventures. Or at least that's what Dat says.

Love, Mem

Caleb folded up the letter and returned it to the envelope. It was just as he'd thought. Talk of the crops, of cleaning, and of loss. Guilt constricted his lungs and made it hard to breathe.

And here he was, heading out on a wagon trip while his father worked their farm alone. *Ja*, his brothers-in-law offered help, but not the help a son should be giving. And where would he be if he returned, living the type of life his *opa* had warned him about? He'd seen the regret in his grandfather's face and didn't want to become the weary and worried old man he'd been before the stroke.

This is my time. His mem had said it plain. The only thing better about the adventure of the next few weeks would be having someone to join him on it.

Caleb folded his arms and spoke into the room lit by the brightening rays, staring at Amos' bunk. "Do you think Rebecca would be interested in coming on the wagon ride?"

"*Hummpf?*" From the growl of Amos' voice, it was clear he was done talking.

"I know she just got here, but it wouldn't hurt to ask, would it?" He smiled, wondering again where she'd gotten that spunk. He'd also like to know how come she wasn't already married. Surely someone like her would have caught the eye of an Amishman long ago.

Caleb grabbed three shirts from the stack Ruth Sommer had washed for him and tucked those into the duffel. Marianna's mem sometimes took in laundry, and rumor had it if one stopped by to pick up his things around dinnertime, he'd be invited in for a meal. Caleb had found that to be true.

"Rebecca did say she was coming tonight." He spoke more to himself than Amos. He rubbed his chin, in need of a shave. He just needed to think of a stunt that would capture her attention . . . and hold it. And if he could get Marianna to encourage her friend to go along, well, that would be even better.

CHAPTER

8

For the last three years Rebecca had slept fitfully most nights. She often woke while others slept, planning when she'd leave and where she'd go. And the only thing that had calmed her—that had made her willing to push through another day, focusing on her schooling and trying to ignore her lies—was that she *could* go. Only one other person had known of her dream. And that person had made everything possible.

Rebecca sat on the floor, pulling her suitcase toward her. She'd emptied her things into the dresser in the room, but while the suitcase looked empty, it held Rebecca's peace inside. Her eyes fluttered closed, and then she moved her fingers to the hidden flap. Mem had forced her to sew, yet she'd had no idea how Rebecca's best handiwork would be used.

Pulling back the bottom edge of the lining revealed a hidden zipper. Unzipping it, Rebecca slid her hand inside. The pounding of her heart stilled as her fingers touched the edge of paper. Unable to hold back any longer, Rebecca pulled out the small stack of money. Ten thousand dollars. Her grandmother's life savings.

"You know I never have trusted banks," her grandmother had said more than once when she visited.

"I don't think most people your age do, *Oma*," Rebecca had often responded.

"The banks failed before, and they could fail again." *Oma* had spoken with sternness. "Besides, we should never put into man's hands what God has intended us to use for His good."

If her grandma had said the same thing one time, she'd said it one hundred. And then, one year ago, just a few weeks before her grandmother's death, her *oma* had refused to allow Rebecca to just listen and nod.

"Aren't you going to ask me what I meant by that?" *Oma* had said.

"By what?"

"Well, what I meant by putting into man's hands what God meant for good."

"I thought it was just a saying."

Oma had tsk-tsked her then. "Young woman, maybe you thought that, but don't you want to ask?"

"Ask what?"

"Well, if I haven't trusted banks all these years, don't you want to ask what I did with all the money I saved? All the money that's not in a bank?"

"You saved money?" Rebecca had glanced around the room. "Is it in here?"

A sparkle from Grandma's eye lightened Rebecca's heart. Even with her health declining, her grandmother always had a quick wit about her.

"*Ja*, and I will tell you where. But first I need you to tell me what you've been doing with those school books."

Rebecca's heart had skipped a beat. "You . . . saw me?"

"Darling girl, do you think a grandmother really sleeps

fifteen hours a day? Sometimes I just pretended to sleep so you could get your work done."

"It's college work, *Oma*. I know you'll be mad—"

"Is it nursing?" *Oma* had attempted to sit up straighter, but there was hardly any muscle on her thin frame, and she sank back into the pillows. "I read that on one of the spines."

"*Ja*, a delivery nurse . . . for babies." On one hand Rebecca couldn't believe she was telling her grandmother the truth. On the other hand, in a strange way she'd felt *Oma* would understand. Her grandmother lived the life of a good Amish woman, but she also seemed less concerned about the opinions of others than most people Rebecca knew. Maybe it was because *Oma* also spent more time reading the Bible than others in Rebecca's family. It was as if she found an internal strength there that allowed her not to get overly worried about external things.

Tears had trailed down her grandmother's cheeks. "It's because of Claudia, isn't it?"

"*Ja* . . ." She'd only had enough strength to offer one word.

"Your parents will be disappointed."

Rebecca nodded.

"With me as well as you."

"What do you mean?"

"*Liebling*, go to my trunk and unfold my kitchen aprons. I've never thrown one away. There should be ten of them, and in the pocket of each one are ten one-hundred-dollar bills."

Rebecca reached over and touched her grandmother's forehead. Surely she was feverish and disillusioned.

"If you think I'm out of my mind, maybe I am. But I loved Claudia too. I've also never known a more tender nurse than you. I want you to have the money. But promise me one thing . . ."

"*Ja*?"

"When you return—and you *will* return to repent—say a prayer for me too. Say a prayer that your mem won't be too mad at me for both hiding the money and helping her daughter."

"I—I always pray for you." And that was the truth. Even when she couldn't pray for herself, she could always pray for *Oma*. "But . . . why would you do this, when you know I'll be educating myself in the ways of the world?"

"I trust you, Rebecca. I trust you."

Even now those words filled Rebecca's soul with a sense of peace. Those words were one of the last things *Oma* had said to her.

Months later in class, Rebecca learned that some people get a burst of energy before they decline and die, and she was thankful her grandma hadn't stopped with those words alone. She liked to think of her grandmother's last words as more of a last blessing rather than part of the natural process.

"I trust your heart. I trust your motives. Some may not want your help yet. Some may allow their worries to overshadow their needs. But if there's one thing I've learned in my seventy-five years, it's that change will happen. Years ago I wouldn't have dreamed of having a phone in the phone shed not far from the house, but we've come to accept it. Maybe not in my lifetime, but hopefully in yours, people will start to see that not all changes are bad. And not all steps toward the world will bring damnation to one's soul. Promote healing, Rebecca. And as you do this, it'll mean your healing will come too."

Now, sitting on the cold wood floor while birds chirped on the branches of a pine tree just outside her window, Rebecca held the money tightly, pressing it against her heart. She didn't know how many eggs *Oma* had sold for this, but without it— and the scholarships she'd received—she wouldn't be able to venture out. Was what *Oma* said true? Would the schooling help her own heart? Would it mend up the hole her sister had left? Would it calm the fear she felt every time a family member or friend announced that a baby was on the way?

Rebecca hoped that to be true.

After returning the money to the hidden compartment and getting herself ready for the day, Rebecca quietly walked through the living room and stood far enough back so Ben and Marianna couldn't see her through the window from their place at the garden. Ben held a cup of steaming coffee in his hand, and he listened and chuckled as Marianna chatted about something as she weeded.

How long had they been up? From the signs of the breakfast dishes drying on the rack behind her, it had to be a few hours at least. A better question was how had she slept so long? The quiet was the main reason, she supposed. Back home her dat was up at four o'clock. His banging around as he lit the woodstove served as an alarm clock for the rest of the family. But here it was quiet. There wasn't the sound of children. There were no busy roads or the sounds of trucks and buggies.

She watched Ben, who was wearing jeans and a plain blue T-shirt. It was clear why Marianna had fallen for him, and she knew what Ben saw in Marianna, but what about her? Would anyone ever look at her with adoration in his gaze? By leaving the Amish, she'd be leaving behind any hopes of finding love. An Amishman wouldn't love someone who'd left. Yet she was too Amish—too Plain—to get the attention of an *Englischer.*

Rebecca found muffins on the counter, and she poured herself a glass of orange juice from the fridge. She sat at the table and flipped through the newspaper, wondering when they were going to come in. Didn't they have church today?

Thirty minutes later the two entered, faces aglow, strolling as if they didn't have a care in the world.

Rebecca looked at the clock. "I thought you were leaving for church today."

"Ben and I talked about it, and we are going to stay home. We don't know how long you'll be with us, and we'd rather spend time talking with you."

"Is that allowed?" Rebecca dared to ask.

Ben settled across from her at the table in one of the kitchen chairs. "What do you mean?"

"Do you have to confess before the church if you skip?"

Ben chuckled. "*Ne*, it's nothing like that. We know that God desires for us to join together to worship and to unite with other believers, but we also live under grace. Jesus got into trouble for picking heads of wheat on the Sabbath and allowing others to do the same. The Jewish religious leaders accused Him of going against God's laws, but He *was* God. I think He was showing us that what we often make a big deal of isn't that big of a deal at all."

Rebecca nodded, pretending she understood, but wondering what wheat had to do with missing church. "So we're all staying home?"

Ben nodded. "Marianna's going to pack a picnic lunch, and I'll bring my Bible. There's a story about a Samaritan I think you'll like."

"He tended the injured man when the religious leaders walked by. *Ja*, I've read that before."

"Good! Then we can have a lively discussion!"

Less than an hour later they were sitting on the shore of Carpenter Lake. At first Marianna didn't understand why they drove past the large Lake Koocanusa to come here, but once they got out of the car she understood. This lake was small, intimate. Except for a few fishermen, they were the only ones there. Soft green grass lined the shore, and the sound of the lapping water brought a smile to Rebecca's face.

Beyond the trees on the other shoreline was a mountain range. Rebecca was certain she'd never take those mountains for granted as long as she stayed here.

"Rats. Should have brought my fishing pole." Ben slapped his leg with his hat as he climbed from the truck.

"Sorry, you'll just have to sit with us and suffer through all the small talk," Marianna chirped.

"Well, as long as you packed up some of those raspberry bars that you made, then it's a deal."

Soon a soft gray blanket was spread, and each had a plate full of chicken salad sandwiches, carrot sticks, blueberry muffins, and the oatmeal raspberry bars that looked delicious. They sat there, enjoying the meal and view and small talk, until Marianna turned the subject to something Rebecca had avoided. "So how are things back in the community?" she asked.

"The same, I suppose. Does anything ever really change in Shipshewana?"

"*Vell*, my sister-in-law Naomi wrote and told me they painted the school. It was white but someone messed up and it's more off-white now." Marianna chuckled. "I miss it, you know. I mean, as much as I love it here—love Ben—Indiana still feels like home. I suppose it always will."

"It doesn't seem right that someone else is living in your family's old house. Things look different. I suppose they'll never really be the same again. *Ach*, and another change that will always happen: more babies have been born. Do you remember Eleanor Lapp, who was a year ahead of us in school? She just had her third *boppli*. Can you believe it?"

Marianna grabbed a muffin and slowly peeled off the paper wrapper, as if it captured all her attention, but Rebecca could see that her mind was someplace else.

"So do they ever talk about me?" Marianna finally asked.

"Of course, don't they talk about everyone who leaves?" Rebecca offered a harsh chuckle. "And they believe your parents will be next. They think that's why you came here—to hide your actions. They believe that you want to get away from the eyes of the community so you can live like you want. They think it's easier for you—your parents—to walk away."

Tears rimmed Marianna's eyes. "They have no idea. It was the hardest thing I've ever done. It's still hard. That's who I was . . . and the only thing that made me know that it was time for me to go was what—who—I had waiting." Marianna glanced up at Ben, but instead of the look of love she expected to see exchanged between them, Marianna's eyebrows knotted in worry. Ben saw it too.

"Are you all right?" He reached out and touched her arm.

Marianna shrugged. "My stomach is hurting, that's all."

Ben's face went pale. "I think we better head for home. As great as this has been, you need to rest."

Marianna stood, and it was Ben who set to work cleaning up their lunch things.

"Oh, *ja*. We should rest before Edgar's party." Marianna tried to keep her tone light.

Rebecca could tell something was wrong, but neither Ben nor Marianna gave any hints as to what it was. Instead she followed their cue and stayed silent most of the trip home. As much as Ben and Marianna tried to pretend they had the perfect life, something was definitely bothering them.

CHAPTER

9

Even though she'd slept in until almost eight o'clock, Rebecca didn't have a hard time dozing off when she lay down for a nap. Her mother had always told her she was gone too much and needed time to rest. Back home she hadn't had the option. In addition to her work and family, the few extra hours of her free time were spent on school work.

Rebecca brushed out her hair and then carefully pinned it up so that not one stray piece was out of place. Fortunately, Marianna still had all her Amish clothes. Rebecca borrowed a blue dress, stockings, and a vest and apron. The dress was the same dark blue as the lupines that dotted her dat's farmland in the spring. Her *kapp* was white, pressed to perfection.

Marianna still looked a little pale when they climbed into the truck again, but she seemed to be doing better now than she had been. It took only five minutes for them to drive by truck to Marianna's parents' house. The Sommer family lived in a log house not far down the road from the Kootenai Kraft and Grocery and the small Amish school. Ben parked the truck, and right away Rebecca noted a mix of buggies and vehicles parked there.

"I wouldn't believe such a place existed if—" Rebecca's words caught in her throat as she noticed someone approaching.

Caleb jogged down the front porch steps and headed their direction. "Marianna, yer dat saw you pull up and was headed out to give you all a hand, but I told him to let me do the honors."

Ben had already pulled out the large cooler filled with a jug of sun tea and a cut watermelon and was carrying that to the house. Caleb grabbed the lawn chairs.

"That's awful kind of you." Marianna glanced at Rebecca. "I'm sure Rebecca would love to follow you around back, Caleb. She hasn't been to my folks' place yet."

"*Ja*, of course." He glanced back at her and smiled. "If you'd like to follow."

Rebecca had no choice but to match his stride. She should have talked to Marianna. She should have reminded her that she wasn't interested in being paired up. And why would Marianna think she would be? She'd seen Rebecca as she climbed off the train wearing *Englisch* clothes. Did that give Marianna confidence that Rebecca was prepared for an Amish relationship? Then again, she was wearing Amish clothes now. Maybe that gave Marianna hope.

In the backyard, tables and chairs were set up. A trailer was off to the side. "I see they are using the items from the church's bench wagon. I'm not sure if I've ever seen our community's benches used like that."

"What do you mean?" Caleb asked.

"*Vell*, back in Indiana, church benches are used for church, and I wouldn't call having a birthday party for an *Englisch*man anything related to church."

"My, isn't someone prepared to have a good time? Is there something else you want to mention before we kick off our shoes and join the game?" Rebecca followed Caleb's gaze to the young people playing volleyball in one corner of the yard. She gasped as she realized they had indeed kicked off their shoes and were playing barefooted—teens in *Englisch* and Amish clothes together.

Rebecca gazed up at Caleb. "Are you asking me to play? I—"

"Rebecca!"

She heard the familiar voice calling her name and turned to see Ruth Sommer approaching. The woman's hair had grown grayer around the temples. Had Marianna's leaving the Amish church had anything to do with that?

"Mrs. Sommer!" Rebecca rushed forward. She was surprised when the older woman offered her a quick hug.

"You can call me Ruth, dear. You're not a little girl anymore. I was worried when Marianna told me you were on your way here, alone, but Abe reminded me that God holds you in the palm of His hand, just like He holds the rest of our kids."

Rebecca smiled. "*Ja, vell,* what is life without adventure?"

Out of the corner of her eye she noticed Caleb standing there and knew she shouldn't say more than that. Maybe— hopefully—she'd have time to sit down with the Sommer family and catch up.

"I'm glad you mentioned adventure." Caleb took a step forward, and Rebecca was surprised that he was jumping into their conversation. From the look on Mrs. Sommer's face, she was too.

Caleb cleared his throat. "Rebecca, I know you came to visit your friend, but we have a trip we're going to take. Ben and Marianna were going to go, but they changed their mind. We have space. It's a full week there and back to Libby, but it's something you'll never get a chance to experience again. We'll be taking our wagons and buggies along old logging roads in the mountains. Some guys I know did the same trip a few years back, and they said it was like being on the Oregon Trail. Of course the mountains are different. There are beautiful mountain ranges that I'm sure you'd love to see—"

"Wait." Rebecca held up a hand. "Are you inviting me to go with you?"

"It's not just me. There is Amos, Marianna's uncle Ike, and two womenfolk, Annie and Millie."

Laughter burst from Ruth's lips. "Now that's quite a traveling party if I ever heard of one."

"Well, I don't know . . . I feel bad that Ben and Marianna have chosen not to go. It does sound like a fun trip. Maybe if we all went . . ."

"Oh no, dear." Mrs. Sommer shook her head. "The doctor in Kalispell told Marianna she needs to rest. With her spotting . . . Well, we don't want to risk anything happening to this *boppli*." Ruth placed a hand over her mouth, as if just remembering she wasn't supposed to say anything.

"*Boppli*?" The word escaped with Rebecca's breath as if someone had just punched her in the gut. "There's a baby?"

The color drained from Ruth's face, and she looked to Caleb—as if he could do anything to help her take back her words.

"Oh my, I thought you knew," Ruth said. "Maybe Marianna was just worried. I mean, maybe she didn't want to worry you. After all . . . all that you've been through in your family. With your sister."

Rebecca nodded, but she didn't know what to say. What could she say? Maybe Marianna was trying to protect her, but why would she hide such a thing from her best friend?

"How far along is she?" she dared to ask.

"Eleven weeks. The other two babies were lost during this time."

"Other two?" The pain came unexpectedly and tears sprang to Rebecca's eyes. Suddenly her head ached, and the voices of those playing volleyball seemed too loud. They pounded through her temples.

"I am so sorry." Ruth's worried eyes fixed on Rebecca's. "I should have talked to Marianna about all of it. Marianna is a private person. Not many people know what's happening, but you are such a close friend. I just assumed—"

"Sometimes distance does that." Rebecca shrugged, trying to keep her tone light. "It's not something easy to talk about over the phone, and I can see how a letter wouldn't do it justice."

Yet she thought about the last few days. There had been numerous chances for Marianna to spill her heart. The pain of betrayal stabbed at her. Rebecca glanced at the volleyball that sailed through the air again, far out of bounds. It veered toward the roof, hit the wooden shingles, and clattered down. Laughter followed the ball, and she again questioned what she was doing there.

Rebecca glanced at Caleb. He stood silent, unsure of what to say. What to do. From the corner of her eye Rebecca noticed Marianna settling into one of the lawn chairs. Her eyes filled with moisture, and she thought about the pain her friend must be experiencing, losing not one but two babies . . . and now having worries about the third.

Rebecca blew out a breath and turned to Caleb. "Can I think about the trip? How soon do you need to know?"

He offered a soft smile. "We're leaving bright and early Monday morning. You wouldn't need to bring anything but yourself. Between everyone else we have enough camping supplies. But if you need it, I can give you five, or maybe ten, minutes to decide." He winked.

Rebecca turned to Mrs. Sommer, hoping she'd give some input. Instead the older woman motioned to the table with the cake.

"It's getting late. I should cut the cake. I know Edgar has been waiting to taste it. Carrot cake is his favorite."

Children ran and played around the yard, and for a moment Rebecca wished she could be one of them again. How carefree she and Marianna used to be. They'd run and played with the other children after service. They'd snuck apples from the cellar and read to each other under the covers with a flashlight that was supposed to be used for emergencies only. But now the innocent days were gone. Even though things seemed fine between them, Marianna obviously didn't trust her. Hiding the truth about her pregnancy was proof of that. The more time spent together, the more Rebecca realized how far apart they'd grown. She couldn't imagine awkward day following awkward day to come.

She glanced up at Caleb. "I think I'd like to go."

Caleb didn't respond, but a large smile filled his face. He kicked against a pinecone on the ground and then turned to her. "I'm glad you said that. The wilderness . . . Well, it's different than back east, you know."

She chuckled and looked back to the wooded area behind the Sommer family's house. "*Ja*, I can see that. There seems to be a lot of places to explore. My little brother Claude would love it so." Emotion filled her throat as she said her brother's name, and she hoped Caleb didn't notice. She turned back to him.

"Are you enjoying yourself?" Caleb asked. "Being in Montana?"

"*Ja, danki*. Everyone is nice. I know now why the Sommer family decided to move here for good. The people here are kind."

"*Ja*, I think so too." He studied her with bright blue eyes. "They have a special kindness about them, and an element of adventure."

"Like you?" She chuckled. "You were pretty brave encouraging me to get behind the steering wheel of that big truck. I could have run you over. More than that, I saw your diving yesterday."

His eyes widened. "You were there?"

"Well, I might have been watching from the truck when Marianna delivered lunch."

Caleb's brow furrowed slightly. Then he grinned and pointed to a nearby tree. "Yeah, the shortest cliff is about as tall as the tallest tree in the cluster. Can you believe I jumped that far?"

"*Ne*, I can't." She chuckled, thinking how Caleb acted strangely similar to her twelve-year-old *bruder* Isaiah, especially when he was excited. "But . . . I don't think you should do that again. Do you know if your body twisted just a little bit in the wrong direction you could break your neck and be in a wheelchair for life? I've read about people getting serious injuries from far less."

"You've read about it? What type of reading do you do?"

Rebecca pressed her lips together. "*Ach*, things here and there. You know . . ." She was trying to think of what else to say when the volleyball sailed through the air out of bounds. It bounced up onto the roof again, but instead of rolling down, this time it wedged in the place where a tree branch touched the top of the roof.

Laughter erupted, and the young people teased Charlie

about his serve. Charlie was one of Marianna's brothers, and Rebecca smiled as he teased them back. He looked about two inches taller since the last time she'd seen him, which was before the Sommer family ever left for Montana. So many changes had happened since then. Life moved on whether she liked it or not.

"Are you saying that was out of bounds?" Charlie chuckled. "Can I dispute it?" The boy, who must be nearing the age of twelve or so, waved a hand. "Don't worry. I'll get a ladder."

"No need for that!" Caleb waved at him, then hurried over. "I can get it."

As if in slow motion, Caleb climbed onto the porch railing, reached up to the roof, and then hoisted himself up as easily as if a rope were lifting him upward. Without looking back, or looking down, he stood on the roof and walked up to the ball, lifted it from the branch, and tossed it down.

Cheers arose as it rolled off the roof and Charlie caught it. Caleb then walked down the roof, sat on the edge with his legs dangling, and jumped off.

"I do think someone was showing off for you." It was Marianna's voice. Rebecca hadn't realized her friend had walked over and stood next to her.

"Didn't you say yourself that Caleb did stuff like that?"

"*Ja*, but I've never seen him look back at a young woman, *ach*, about four times, during a stunt."

"I hope you don't mind—I've agreed to go with him on the wagon ride."

Marianna nodded. She rubbed her arm, as if suddenly getting a chill, and offered Rebecca the slightest of smiles. "I think you'll have a great time."

They stood in awkward silence for a moment, and Marianna placed a soft hand on her stomach.

Rebecca noticed and leaned close to her friend, talking low. "You should have told me about the *boppli*—about the babies."

Shock registered on Marianna's face. Her mouth opened slightly, and then her voice emerged in no more than a whisper. "It seems as if we've both been keeping secrets."

"When did it come to this?" Rebecca asked.

Marianna sighed. "That doesn't seem to be the right question. Even when I was in Indiana, you hid the truth from me. I saw you nearly every day, and you hid the truth. And then, when I moved to Montana, I hid the truth from you. In my letters I didn't tell you about my attraction to Ben. How could I have ever explained that my heart was being drawn to a musician? One secret leads to another, doesn't it? A better question seems to be, why did we ever think that it wouldn't come to this?"

They stood side by side as her father started a bonfire. On the table a large cake was being sliced into pieces, and the older man, Edgar, had a wide smile, no matter how hard he tried to straighten it.

Marianna released a sigh and turned to her. "I'm sorry I didn't tell you the truth. I want to be excited about this baby, but I'm afraid. I was going to tell you over the next few days. Especially after Ben told me he already told some of his friends. I knew you'd be mighty upset if you heard it from a bachelor!"

Rebecca placed a hand on her hip. "*Ja*, I would have. Men don't understand, do they?"

"Ben is full of faith. He truly believes this baby will be all right. That's one thing I love about him. He trusts God." Marianna crossed her arms over her chest. "I hope he's right, and I don't want your thoughts of me to keep you from a once-in-a-lifetime experience."

"So you don't mind if I go on the wagon trip?"

"*Ne*, it's probably better. I started spotting this afternoon and called the doctor. He wants me to do as little as possible over the next few days. I'm not going to be any fun."

Spotting? A pain shot through her chest and fears clawed deep inside as she remembered Mrs. Sommer saying the same thing. She tried to push the fear down. Surely everything was going to be all right. God wouldn't do this to Marianna again. Surely He wouldn't . . .

"I could stay with you." She tried to keep her tone light. "We can quilt."

Marianna cocked an eyebrow. "Or . . . you can go and get to know Caleb a little better. He's a bit on the wild side, but he's a nice guy. I'm not sure how close his relationship with God is . . . but it's something you can find out."

Rebecca wanted to say, "Ja, *well, I don't know how close my relationship is with God—so that makes two of us.*" Instead she just nodded. "Deep down I'm telling myself that I don't need this," she said. "Don't need the complication of being attracted to someone."

"But you're still going to go?"

Rebecca twisted her *kapp* string around her finger. "*Ja.* When was the last time I ever paid attention to common sense?"

"*Gut.* And we still have tonight to catch up. I want to hear all about those classes you've been taking. And I might just bore you with the whole story of our romance." She chuckled. "Then you'll surely be ready to head for the hills after that!"

CHAPTER

10

The sun had barely peeked over the highest mountains outside her window when Rebecca hauled her suitcase out of the bedroom. Inside were all her belongings, including the money she had tucked away. She'd considered leaving it in Marianna's home, but there were only two options. The first was to tell Marianna and ask her to hold the money, but that would bring up too many questions. The second was to hide it, but what if it was found? She'd still have to explain. No, her only option was to cart it with her. Then, at least, she could keep an eye on it and not have to confess that her grandmother had been in on her scheme.

She was wearing her Amish dress that she'd washed the night before. Thankfully Marianna also had a dryer, which made things simple.

Marianna sat on the couch with a quilt over her lap. She was wearing pajamas, and her hair was up in a ponytail. Her Bible was open, and a sweet smile graced her lips. "Hey, there. Are you excited about your adventure?"

"*Ja*, I have to say I am. I still feel bad leaving you."

"Actually, I'm feeling better. I stopped cramping and spotting, so things are good. My doctor thinks it was stress."

"Stress? Did I really stress you out showing up?"

"You didn't, but maybe my worries about what you would think about me did. I mean, I know I told you to come anytime, but deep down I didn't think you would—at least not this soon. I was worried what you would think of my house."

"Are you kidding? It's beautiful."

"*Ja*, and we also have electric lights and a dishwasher, a phone and a dryer too." Marianna lowered her head and fiddled with a thread on the quilt. "And I wasn't going to say anything, but we also have a television. But I made Ben carry it downstairs and hide it."

Rebecca sat on the couch next to Marianna's feet. "And what did he say about that?"

"He said we live under grace and not law. He said as followers of Christ our goal is to live like Jesus did and not worry about man-made laws. He said we should strive for purity, not conformity."

A burden sat heavy on Rebecca's shoulders as she listened to those words. The smile on her face faded. "Is that what you think I'm doing: conforming?" She touched her *kapp* self-consciously.

"*Ne.*" The word shot from Marianna's lips. "I didn't mean it to sound that way—"

"But that is what I'm doing. I showed up in an *Englisch* skirt, and now I'm back in Amish dress."

"Maybe so, but what one wears is between oneself and God. He should be the One who guides us, who directs His will for us. In fact . . ." She pointed to a large paper bag with handles sitting on the kitchen counter. "I packed up more of my Amish clothes for you. I know you left most of your things at home, and I thought you would like these. You can ask Ben. I wore my Amish clothes—even my *kapp*—for months after we were married. It's hard to change too quickly. It might seem the right thing to do, but who says that everything has to change overnight? I don't advise it.

"Being Amish was my identity—was your identity—for so long," Marianna continued. "Just seek God and let Him guide you. Trust Him, not a hasty decision. There's a Scripture verse that talks about God's mercies being new every morning. I'm thankful they are, and I'm thankful I don't have to figure it all out myself. I'm not who I was . . . but I know I'm not close to who I can be in God, either."

"And now?" Rebecca pointed to Marianna's ponytail. "Are you going to stop wearing a head covering completely?"

"*Ach*," Marianna gasped. She patted her head. "I forgot I wasn't wearing one. Sometimes I do, and sometimes I don't. And can I tell you a secret?"

"*Ja*."

"Well, the reason I often wear one is because that's the only way I know how to fix my hair. Ben insists I can get it cut and styled . . . but that seems like it would take so much time."

Rebecca nodded and looked to the paper bag. Part of her wanted to tell Marianna that she'd only take her own things. Then she'd have to force herself to wear *Englisch* clothes along the way, and to confess to Caleb what her plans were. But the other part of her . . . Well, she mostly wanted to enjoy the next week. To enjoy being an Amish young woman who was being pursued by an Amish young man. She wanted to forget that soon everything—her whole life—would change.

"*Ja*, dressing Amish is easier, I suppose. No decisions." Rebecca picked up the paper bag and opened the suitcase, placing the Amish clothes inside.

"You can leave what you don't need here. I mean, if you want to take a smaller bag with just what you need, instead of your whole suitcase."

"No," Rebecca answered quickly. "I'm going to take it all . . . just in case. If I don't, I'm sure I'll forget something."

"And you don't need anything else? A sleeping bag? A flashlight?"

Rebecca shook her head. "*Ne*. Caleb said that someone named Millie would be bringing everything else I need, even a jacket for the cool nights."

"Millie is great." Marianna sat straighter. "You're going to love her. In fact, I see her truck coming up the road."

Marianna rose and walked Rebecca to the door. "You'll have fun, and I'm going to try to talk Ben into meeting the wagon train in Libby. It's only an hour or two by car."

Rebecca nodded. "That would be fun." She wanted to tell Marianna that if her parents called, to not admit she was here, but it would be no use. Marianna would tell the truth no matter what.

They walked out the door as the truck parked. Rebecca didn't know what she was expecting, but the stocky older woman with white hair permed into tight curls and the swagger of a cowboy wasn't it. The woman's face was a map of wrinkles, and she wore a wide smile.

"There ya are, sweetheart. Are you ready to go? Everything else is already at the store all loaded up. Now we're just waiting for our most precious cargo." Millie stretched out her hand. She shook Rebecca's firmly and then grabbed the suitcase. When it was loaded in the back of her pickup truck, Millie pointed her thumb to the passenger seat. "Load 'em up!"

"I guess that means time to go."

"*Ja*, and Millie's not one to wait." Marianna patted

Rebecca's shoulder. "I'll see you in a few days, if we're able to make it to Libby."

Rebecca climbed into the truck. "*Ja*, I'll like that!" She'd barely shut the door when Millie started the engine and put the truck into gear, heading in the direction of the store.

"I'm glad you're coming. It'll give those bachelors someone pretty to look at instead of an old crow like me."

"I'm glad, too, but I'm pretty certain I don't know what I'm getting myself into."

Millie's chuckle was deep and raspy. "I've lived enough years on this earth to know that it's okay not to know. That's part of the adventure, and it's what trusting God is all about. I've spent many years learnin'." And that one comment was all Millie needed to launch into her life. By the time they pulled up to the West Kootenai Kraft and Grocery, Rebecca knew more about Millie's parents than she'd ever heard about her own grandparents.

When the truck stopped, Rebecca jumped out and retrieved her suitcase from the back. With a grin, Caleb stepped forward to introduce her around. "Rebecca, you know Amos already, and now Millie. I wanted you to meet Annie and Ike." The two stood side by side, close enough that Rebecca thought there was a special friendship between them, but no closer than that. Rebecca understood why. Ike was an Amish bachelor in his midforties, she'd guess. No one would approve of his having a special relationship with a single *Englisch* woman. No one.

"Uncle Ike, I believe we met a few times when I was a child yet. I'm Marianna's friend who never could keep her hair controlled and tucked under her *kapp*. I'm pretty sure that during the summer I never wore a pair of shoes." She chuckled. "In fact, I'd hear from my mem all the time—she was so worried, I guess, that the neighbors would think I didn't *own* a pair."

"*Ja*, I remember." He stroked his chin. "I'd pick out those large brown eyes anywhere, especially the humor in them." Ike took a step closer and peered down. "*Ja*, I do believe you still have some secrets you're hiding. Let's hope they don't have anything to do with missing peach preserves."

Rebecca felt heat rising to her cheeks and tried to keep her tone light, as if his comment about trying to hide secrets hadn't affected her.

"Oh no, I promise I didn't sneak any of Marianna's preserves and hide them in my suitcase. They still are my favorite, though."

And before he had a chance to probe any more about her secrets, Rebecca turned to the woman standing next to him. She was just about Rebecca's height, and she had a heart-shaped face and a long blond ponytail. She wore jeans, a flannel shirt, and hiking boots. Obviously the dress code up here in Montana.

Rebecca smiled at the woman. "And you must be Annie. Do I remember right that Marianna said you were the owner of the grocery?"

"Yup, that would be me. We're excited you're joining us. Any friend of Marianna's is a friend of mine."

There was a small group of other people standing around in the parking lot to see them off. Caleb stepped forward and took the suitcase from her hand. "I have a spot for this, right in back, next to all the food—the most important stuff."

He walked to a horse-drawn covered wagon that appeared similar to the one on the cover of the Little House on the Prairie books she'd read as a child. There was one other similar wagon, and also a smaller wagon that had large rubber wheels—something that would never be allowed back in Indiana.

Caleb put her suitcase in the back of the first wagon and

then turned to her. "I saved you a seat next to me. I hope you don't mind."

Tingles danced up and down Rebecca's arms. "I, uh, guess not." She looked around, waiting for someone else to object, but no one did.

Caleb offered her a hand. She reluctantly took it, and he helped her into the wagon. A cushion, like the kind people took with them to sit on in the bleachers during Amish baseball games, lay on the seat. Rebecca sat on it, liking the idea that Caleb had thought of it.

"We'll see you in a week, give or take." Caleb climbed aboard. The two other wagons were filled by people and supplies. Amos and Ike were in the first, and Annie and Millie in the second. Everyone was in high spirits, excited by the adventure. Their voices rose, nearly drowning out the sound of the rocks being spit from under the wheels of the first two wagons as they moved out.

"Head out, ho!" Caleb called to their two horses.

The animals started and moved right into an easy pace.

"I think they're a little excited too." He chuckled. "I'll let them get a little energy out, and then we'll settle in."

"I can't believe we're doing this." Rebecca pulled her sweater tighter around her. She didn't know if the shiver she felt moving up and down her spine was from the chill in the air or from sitting next to Caleb. Her body rocked slightly from side to side with the movement of the covered wagon.

They passed the small Amish school, and the children rushed out the door. "Good-bye, good-bye!" they called.

Rebecca waved back. "I feel as if I'm in a parade."

"*Ja*, and just wait until the end of the day. There will be other creatures eyeing us. And of course we'll be eyeing them too."

"What do you mean?"

"You didn't hear? This is the best time of year to see wild-life. Bears especially will be scrounging the forests, looking to fill up their bellies before winter."

"Bears?" Rebecca reached down and gripped the edge of the wooden seat. "You're kidding, *ja*?"

"No. Why would I be kidding? Didn't you look around, Rebecca? We're heading into the wilderness."

Caleb was silent then. He barely held the reins in his hand and instead looked to the sides, taking in the sights of the houses along the roadway. Rebecca did too.

Even though she'd been here in the West Kootenai area for a few days, she hadn't really taken the time to look around. They'd driven around the area in Marianna's truck, and Rebecca had missed so much. It was nice to take everything in at a slower pace. When she was a child, one of her favorite things had been to enjoy time in the buggy with her family, but as she'd gotten older, she'd forgotten that. It had been easier to get rides into town for work from Lora or other friends. And in a strange way, things felt right that she was here with Caleb now, moving at the pace of the horses and wearing Amish dress. If anything, it was a reminder to appreciate what she had. It also gave her the resolve that this was what she wanted to return to after nursing school. She didn't know if her family or community would accept her, but at least she would try.

They passed a house that was in the process of being built. A meadow stretched beyond it, and behind that was the mountain range that rose up from the valley. Pine trees covered its slopes in a beautiful bluish-green color that Rebecca hadn't seen in nature before.

"See that house?" Caleb interrupted her thoughts. "We were working on that for an Amish couple who was planning to move here from back east, but construction stopped when they decided to stay where they were."

"Why did they decide to stay?"

"Well, when we talked to them, it was clear that both of their families didn't approve. They say that it's not good to be so far away from those in your community. They believe it's an excuse to act in ways you shouldn't. To make *Englisch* friends and to indulge in the ways of the world. Everyone thinks that because the place has no bishop, everyone does whatever they please."

"I know. The same things were said about this place when the Sommer family moved here. And then when Marianna decided to leave the Amish and marry Ben, well, that just confirmed what they'd been thinking."

Caleb glanced over at her. "I don't know the family well, but sometimes I wonder if there is some truth behind those rumors. Me and some of the other bachelors came for adventure, but I'm still not sure what draws a family. Life is harder—the weather, the work, making a living. Maybe deep down they do want to test and see what it would be like to live beyond a large community.

"Abe Sommer, Marianna's dat, told us that he was worried about his younger sons following his older son's antics. Yet Levi has joined the church, gotten married, and is raising his own son, but they still haven't returned."

"See? Do you understand what I'm saying, *ja*? People have reasons why they leave their communities back east."

Caleb turned to her, fixing his eyes on hers. Was he wondering about her? Why had she come here? Where was she going? She looked back to the front, watching the swooshing of the horses' tails and waiting for the questions.

Instead Caleb cleared his throat. "It does this community no good when people come here with the true motives of leaving the Amish community and becoming *Englisch*. It just makes it harder for the devoted Amish men and women who want to stay Amish and try to live as dedicated lives as they do back east. I'm sure you won't meet them, though, as many of them have put some distance between themselves and Marianna."

"I'm sure it's hard for everyone to try to figure out who they are apart from the community they grew up in. Change is never easy." Her gut ached. Should she just tell Caleb now? Should she let him know that within a matter of weeks she'd be leaving West Kootenai to go to college and live for a time in the *Englisch* world?

Up ahead the other two wagons had veered off the main road and were crossing a small bridge. There was a lovely creek, and she breathed out a sigh that the other wagons were rounding the bend and going out of view. Even though they couldn't hear this conversation, she felt better about spilling the truth to Caleb without having to think of them.

Her hands quivered and she pushed them against her lap, straightening her shoulders as she did. "Caleb, I'm not sure what you heard about me from Ben or whoever, but—"

"Look!" Caleb's low call interrupted her thoughts. The wagon pulled up to the bridge, and Caleb pointed up the stream. There was a crook in the river, and a portion of it was hidden by tall pines. From behind that crook two moose strolled out—a mother and her baby.

A gasp escaped Rebecca's lips and she held in her squeal. Caleb stopped the wagon, and the horses stamped the ground and looked ahead, as if not wanting to be left behind.

The female moose was dark brown, almost black. Her ears were large and perked up. Her nose was longer than a horse's, with a curved bump on the end. She bent down to the water for a drink, and Rebecca held her breath, hoping their presence didn't scare her away. The calf stood by her side, hardly any taller than her mother's knee. It was lighter brown in color and looked like a mix between a fawn and a pony. As its mother drank, it watched the wagon, staring with wide-eyed wonder.

"I can't believe it . . ." Caleb's words were no more than a whisper. "Do you have a camera?"

Rebecca didn't know how to answer. Was this a test? The moose took one step backward, and she realized she shouldn't worry about his opinion of her having a camera. She wanted a photo to send back home. Her brothers and sisters would get a kick out of that, especially Claude.

"*Ja*, I do, but it's in my suitcase."

Caleb started to rise. "I can get it—"

"No!" Her heart leapt into her throat as she pictured what Caleb would see if he unzipped her suitcase and looked inside. He'd see her *Englisch* clothes. He'd see her nursing books that she'd packed. If she was going to tell him, she'd do it her own way, not by having Caleb eye her Hoosier sweatshirt with a curious look.

A sheepish look came over Caleb's face. "I was going to say I can get it down for you, if that'll help."

"Actually, I think I can reach in and get it." Her neck grew hot. Her hands became sweaty and she pressed them together. "I'll do it. No need for you to get down." Rebecca stepped down from the wagon.

As quietly as she could, she moved to the back of the wagon. The moose calf's ears twitched, but neither moved. As she approached the back of the wagon, Rebecca looked back to see Caleb's eyes on her. And for the moment she almost felt as if she were detached from the person she'd been for the last few years. She hadn't let anyone get close. Hadn't let anyone study her, watch her. She felt vulnerable and out of breath, as if she were sinking underwater without the strength to pull herself up. Yet if this was what opening up felt like, she knew why she'd kept everyone at bay. She could get used to this feeling of being close to someone else. And that was a problem for one whose mind was set on doing her own thing.

She reached into the back of the wagon, unzipped the top of her suitcase, and pulled out the camera. With more quiet steps she made her way back to the front of the wagon. Instead of offering a hand or helping her up, Caleb climbed down. She lifted the camera to turn it on, and her breath escaped.

"Oh no . . ."

"What's wrong?"

"I left the camera on and drained the batteries . . . and I didn't bring extras." She turned to him, realizing for the first time how close he stood to her. "You wouldn't happen to have any, would you?"

Caleb chuckled and put both hands into his pockets. "Nope. Not today. I can't say that was on my packing list."

"*Vell*, I do have my cell phone, uh, that I only used for my boss at work to get ahold of me . . . well, mostly." Even as she said those words, she realized she'd never grabbed it from where she'd plugged it in on the bathroom vanity. Not that she'd been using it; she hadn't checked the phone or text messages since she'd gotten off the train—not that she expected to have many if any at all. Only Lora and a few others even knew she had a phone. "No . . . Oh no. I left my cell phone at Marianna's house too."

"Too bad. It is a beautiful scene." His voice was soft, and it comforted her in a way she hadn't expected.

"I can't believe it." She dropped her hand to her side. "I'm never going to see something like this again in my whole life," she whispered.

"You're right. But you still have your memory. And I have a feeling you won't soon forget."

Caleb stepped behind her. His hands moved to her shoulders, and he gently touched her. "Take it in, Rebecca. Do you smell the pine and the stream? The air is warm, isn't it? And look: amazing creatures. Most people will never see this." His breath was warm on her ear. "It's almost as if the moment was created here, now, for us."

Caleb didn't mention God, but he didn't have to. The sun beamed down on her, and it was almost as if God had joined them, too, urging her to pause and bask in His creation. Her chest filled with heat, warmth. She let her eyes flutter closed—the sun warm on her face. What had she done to deserve being here? What had she done to deserve having this moment when she'd just walked away from the people and community who cared for her most?

"I have a feeling we're going to be friends after this." Caleb dropped his hands. Then he stepped forward, until he stood next to her again. "And the truth is, while you were gazing at that river, those trees, and that moose, I was lookin' at an even prettier scene."

"Caleb." Her throat was tight, and she had to force her words out. "You shouldn't talk like that. You act as if you're *Englisch* or something. I've never heard of such a thing in my life as an Amishman saying such fancy words."

"*Vell*, I'm glad I don't have competition, but the truth is I've never said anything before like what's coming out of my mouth. It's just fitting, that's all. But . . ." His finger shot into the air. "If you ever try to tell anyone that I have a soft side, I'm going to tie you up to a tree, pour honey on you, and wait for the bears to come."

Rebecca mocked horror. "You will? That sounds awful."

She turned, stepped away from him, and climbed up into the wagon. "But, Caleb, having a soft side isn't a bad thing. Women like it."

"You like it, maybe. Most of the Amish women I know wouldn't give me the time of day with talk like that. They would think that anything beyond a day's work is foolish. A waste of time."

With those words a flash of pain crossed his face. He moved around the horses to the other side and climbed into the wagon seat. What had she said? What had she done wrong? Because the gentle Caleb who'd been standing beside her just a minute before was nowhere to be seen as he flipped the reins and signaled for the horses to resume.

"I hope they're not too far ahead." He fixed his gaze on the dirt logging road. "I want to make sure we get there for lunch. Ike said we weren't going too far today."

"Um, there's a problem with that." Rebecca glanced over her shoulder. "We're the ones with all the food."

Caleb moaned and then flicked the reins, encouraging the horses to pick up the pace. "Then we better get going. My stomach is already growling, and I don't want to keep Annie and Millie from making up some good grub."

Rebecca held the useless camera on her lap and wished she could ask him about the change in his attitude. Then again, did it matter? Even though her chest still felt warm from the gentle, thoughtful Caleb of a few minutes ago, it wouldn't change things. Rebecca focused ahead, reminding herself of where she needed to set her sights. It would be too easy to push her plans to the side if her heart got in the way. Then how could she live with herself? It was hard enough knowing that if she'd had just a little bit more knowledge, she could have saved her sister.

CHAPTER

11

By the time they'd caught up with the others, Ike had already built a small fire. Rebecca helped Caleb unhitch the horses and was surprised when he took them to a small, high mountain pasture and released them.

"Aren't you going to tether them?" she asked, stroking the side of the beautiful sorrel named Lily.

"No, they won't wander far." Caleb hooked his thumbs through his suspenders. "There's a nice stream over there and lush grass. They'll be able to graze and drink as needed."

Rebecca and Caleb washed up in the stream and then found their way to camp. Ike had already unloaded the large tub of cooking gear, and Annie was rummaging around through the cooler.

"I know I should have packed sandwiches or something for the first day, but I had too much fun looking through my campfire cookbook," Annie chuckled. "We're a few miles less than we'd planned the first day, but this seems like a nice spot. You don't mind, do you?"

"Nope," Caleb answered. "It does look like a beautiful place. Let me know what you need."

"What I need is that bin with those dry goods. And the one

under it has a few more cooking pots. Also"—she glanced up at them— "do you think you could find some fresh huckleberries? I'd love to have some for tomorrow's pancakes."

"Huckleberries!" Caleb removed his hat and scratched his head. "I'd be surprised to find them. Usually the bears pick them clean."

Rebecca eyed him and then clutched her elbows. "Bears? You're joking."

"Do you think so?"

"No, but that's the problem." She eyed the woods behind them. "I didn't even think those were real berries. Are they good?"

Annie turned to Rebecca. "If you're scared, then Millie can go with you. After all, it'll give the rest of us time to set up our tents." She glanced at Caleb. "You will stay and help Ike with those, won't you?"

The disappointment on Caleb's face was clear. Then he eyed Amos. "*Ja* . . . and without a doubt I can put a tent up faster than him." He pointed to his friend.

The sound of movement in the trees startled Rebecca, and her heartbeat quickened its pace. The older lady was emerging from the woods with a handful of small sticks for the fire. "Did I hear someone calling my name?"

"Yes, we were talking about you, Millie. It seems Rebecca here has never seen or tasted a huckleberry."

"Well, that's a shame. I think we need to do something about it." Millie dropped her pile of sticks next to the campfire pit and headed back into the woods. Rebecca had no choice but to join her. She tried not to hide her disappointment. Why was she so sad that she wasn't hiking around these woods with Caleb? They were only friends, right?

Millie slowed her pace and allowed Rebecca to catch up.

Except for the muted voices behind them, the woods were silent. The air smelled musty, like dirt and earth. Her feet crunched on pinecones that littered the ground. Last year's leaves were partially decomposed and lay like a carpet.

Millie didn't say much, but she pointed out signs of life that Rebecca would have missed. A squirrel high in a tree. A cluster of mushrooms at the base of a stump. Wild roses blooming at the base of a hill.

When Millie started heading up the hill, Rebecca paused. "Uh, don't you think we should stay close to camp? I don't want to get lost. Or if there was a bear . . ."

Millie paused and looked back. "Only to the top of this hill. I can still hear Annie's laughter, which means we're not too far. I promise."

"Have you been here before?"

Millie shook her head. "No, but I know how these forests work." She removed the red handkerchief from around her neck and wiped her brow. "I've been picking huckleberries a long time. They like acidic mountain soil and north-facing hillsides most." She pointed. "See those trees? Pine, larch, spruce? Huckleberries like to hang out with those."

They trudged their way up the mountainside. Well, Rebecca was the one trudging along. Even though Millie was more than twice her age, she had no problem. Rebecca's legs burned. Her chest felt heavy. She struggled for breath, which surprised her.

"I can't—can't be—lieve how out of shape I am."

Millie glanced back over her shoulder. "It's probably the high altitude too. Most people aren't used to it. We're about four thousand feet here."

Rebecca paused, attempting to catch her breath. She put her hand on her hip, wishing the burning would stop. "That makes me feel a little better," she managed to say.

She continued on, and when she got to the top, she found Millie standing next to a cluster of bushes. Rebecca gasped. A few of them had small blackish-purple berries. "Are those huckleberries?"

Millie nodded. She pointed to a few of the branches that were bent or snapped off. "Yes, and it looks like it's been raided in the last few days. My guess is that the bear ate his fill and moved on, but we shouldn't dawdle, just in case."

Rebecca eyed the forest. She didn't see any large bearlike shapes, nor hear any crashing sounds, but that didn't keep her heart from pounding. Millie pulled a small plastic bag from her back pocket.

"*Ach*, good, I was wondering what we were going to put the berries in."

Millie chuckled. "I was a rancher's wife for fifty years. I've learned to always keep a folded-up bag in my back pocket, a bit of twine in my front pocket, and a knife in my boot."

"That's *gut*." Rebecca moved as quickly as she could, plucking off berries and dropping them in the bag. "I'm thankful for that knife . . . to fend off the bear."

Millie looked up at her, eyes wide, as if checking to see if Rebecca was serious.

Rebecca winked.

Millie chuckled. "Yes, if that's the case and I do have to face a bear, then I'm glad I have you here. If one takes on a bear with a pocketknife, she's gonna need a nurse."

"Nurse?" Rebecca's stomach lurched. Her strength drained from her legs, and she sank into a kneeling position—her skirt and apron pressing into the damp ground.

"Yes, a nurse. That's what you've been going to school for, isn't it?"

Rebecca's mouth circled into an O. "How did you know?"

"Was I not supposed to know? You seem surprised."

"Well, I wasn't telling too many people. In fact, my parents don't even know. I haven't the nerve to tell them the truth."

"I heard from Susan Carash. She's caring for my horses when I'm gone, and she happened to mention it."

"*Ach*, I see."

"Are you trying to hide the fact that you're going to be starting college next month? Are you saying Caleb doesn't know?"

"Well, I haven't really said anything. I mean we're just new friends, and I have a feeling that if I did mention it, he would think I'd want his input, or I'm trying to include him in my plans for the future."

Millie cocked her head and looked more intensely into Rebecca's eyes. "So you're not sweet on him?"

"I think he's really nice." Rebecca looked down on her lap where a huckleberry had dropped, hoping Millie believed that was all she felt. But the truth was she'd enjoyed the day, and more than once—as they were riding along—she'd imagined what it would be like to sit by Caleb's side more often.

"I can see on your face that you're starting to have feelings. If there's anything to that, then you know what you need to do."

Rebecca lifted her gaze again and resumed her plucking. After she dropped a few dozen berries into the bag, she tossed a few more into her mouth. She bit down, and the firmness of the skin gave way to a juice that tasted like a mix of grapes and blueberries. Sweetness filled her mouth, but it still didn't dissolve the tension in her stomach. "No wonder the bears love them."

"The truth is sweet too." Millie's words were spoken like those of a tender mother to her child.

"I will tell him. When the time is right. It's not like I

planned for any of this to happen. I'd just been planning to go straight to Portland and begin my new life."

"Well, it seems like God had another plan." Millie rose and lifted the bag, which was a quarter full of berries. "This is enough for pancakes, don't you think? We'll leave the rest for the bears. They'll need them to get plumped up for the winter."

Rebecca stood, plucked off a few more berries and popped them into her mouth, then followed Millie back down the hill—her feet stepping into Millie's footprints to ensure good footing.

"You got more than you bargained for, that's for sure."

"I agree . . . I think everyone will be pleased with our bounty."

"No." Millie picked up a few small pinecones and held them in her hand. "I'm not talking about the huckleberries. You came to Montana to see Marianna, and you ended up with all of us. Now here you're on a trip, and you're going to be able to see one of my favorite places—Kootenai Falls and the swinging bridge."

"Kootenai Falls?"

Millie paused. "Do you mean that Caleb didn't tell you where we were going?"

"On a wagon ride. That's all I know."

Millie laughed. "Usually Caleb is focused on the destination and on being first. But it sounds as if this time he's more focused on the journey . . . and who's sitting by his side. All of us were amazed that he didn't mind his wagon trailing behind today."

Rebecca's lungs burned again, but this time it was from holding her breath. "I think that you're making too much of it—making too much of us, Millie—but I am excited about the falls. I've always loved them. And I've never been to a swinging bridge!"

They made it off the hill and started walking back through the thicker treed area. "Maybe I am making much of nothing, or maybe not." Millie paused and held up one of the pinecones between two fingers. "Rebecca, will you take a look at this? All those little nubs hide a seed. That means just *one* of these pinecones has the potential to create a forest. Isn't that amazing that God did that? *His* potential . . . you just never know."

As they walked, the scent of food cooking met them, and the voices grew louder. Rebecca's heart skipped a beat when she heard Caleb's chuckle.

Millie whistled under her breath. "Don't those elk burgers smell good?"

"Elk?" Rebecca slowed her steps slightly.

"You've never eaten elk before? What about moose?"

Rebecca cleared her throat. "I'm pretty sure I've had neither."

"Wonderful. Then this whole trip will be an adventure for you! Personally I love elk, especially with extra ketchup."

CHAPTER

12

After dinner, they finished setting up camp and then put all their food into plastic totes and hoisted them high up into the trees.

"We don't want to tempt any critters," Amos explained.

Rebecca glanced up at the tree. "That doesn't give me any comfort."

Yet as the evening darkened and they toasted marshmallows around the campfire, Rebecca relaxed. The woods around them were quiet, and even though her stomach was full from dinner, she couldn't help but think about tomorrow's huckleberry pancakes.

"Sitting here, I remember being in Indiana doing the same. I remember sitting alongside Marianna and some of our other friends at Youth Singings. We gathered around a fire just like this."

"With marshmallows?" Annie chuckled.

"*Ja.* Sometimes." Rebecca shrugged and tucked her stick farther into the flames. "Although I haven't been to a singing in over a year—uh, in a while."

Millie didn't roast a marshmallow, but she did listen

intently. "Tell us more about Indiana. That's one place I've never been."

Rebecca told them about Shipshewana, the Amish community there, and all the visitors. "My *oma* said that it used to be a quiet place. Not anymore. Buses of tourists come in, and they enjoy the food, the farms, and always seem to have their cameras out. I think that's why I like Montana. People don't make a spectacle of my Amish dress . . . although I have to admit it did help with tips."

Her new friends chuckled, and Rebecca couldn't believe she'd admitted the last part. "One of my uncles makes rocking chairs," she continued on, "and they're usually sold before he's finished. Sometimes there's even a waiting list."

"I remember your uncle," Ike commented. "He told me before that he'd like to come visit Montana sometime. Is everyone jealous that you got here first?"

Ike's face glowed in the light of the campfire, and Rebecca didn't know how to respond. She'd forgotten that Marianna's uncle had lived around the area, too, before he moved to Montana ten years ago. She'd forgotten that he knew many people there, including members of her family. She'd forgotten that even though the Amish didn't have e-mail or talk much on the phone, news spread from one part of the country to the other with letters that noted concern. She glanced to Millie, wondering if the older woman would tell them the truth if she refused.

"Well, my family . . . They don't really know that this is where I've come. It was time for me to get away, to make some changes in my life . . . I . . ." She swallowed hard, wondering how to say the rest when the rumbling of a motorcycle caught her attention.

"What in the world?" Ike jumped up and moved to the roadway. Caleb and Amos soon followed.

Annie's eyes reflected concern. "Who do you think it is?"

Millie was the only one who didn't seem fazed by it. "I bet it's just some kids who were out joyriding and took a wrong turn. There are all types of dirt roads and trails up here. If you don't know exactly where you're going, it's easy to get lost."

They watched, and sure enough, two dirt bikes came up the road. Ike signaled to them, and they pulled over. The guys talked to the bikers for a while, and then Ike signaled to Annie. A minute later Annie was rummaging through one of the totes. After handing the bikers something, she returned to the fire.

"Just two kids. Got lost and didn't realize they weren't heading the right way, and couldn't understand why their cell phones weren't getting a signal. Thank goodness I'd packed up some protein bars. They hadn't eaten all day."

"That was nice of you to help," Rebecca commented, wondering if the others would remember what they'd last been talking about. Instead Caleb and Amos returned and bid everyone good night.

While Ike said he'd stay up to put out the fire, the rest of them made their way to their tents.

Rebecca climbed inside hers and quickly changed into sweatpants and a sweatshirt. She snuggled into her sleeping bag and turned off her flashlight, trying to process where she was and all that had happened. She'd planned her leaving, her schooling, and her trip . . . but it was amazing how one quick decision to visit Marianna had changed everything. Now here she was sleeping in the middle of the Montana wilderness with strangers who were quickly becoming friends.

Rebecca curled on her side and tucked the small travel pillow under her cheek and remembered something *Oma* had once told her—that even when one set her plans, God determined her path, or something like that. And as she drifted off to sleep, Rebecca determined that the path ahead, the one they'd be traveling over tomorrow, and the next day, and the next day, wouldn't put too big of a wrench in her plans. She'd have to see to that.

Rebecca fought against the darkness, awakening with a charley horse in her leg. "Ah, ouch!" she cried out before she could force her lips closed. She kicked out of her sleeping bag, ignoring the nippy night air, and reached her hands around her sweat-panted leg, but it did no good. Before she realized what was happening, the tent flap unzipped and she could make out the grayed image of Caleb's face.

She reached down and wrapped her hands around her calf. "It's . . . ow . . . a cramp."

"Charley horse?"

She nodded and he motioned for her to turn so he could reach her leg. She released her leg. Strong arms wrapped around her calf; he squeezed and rubbed, working to ease the cramping muscles. She wanted to cry out more, but didn't want to wake the others. Instead Rebecca pressed her lips tight and fought back the tears. It took a few minutes for the spasms to pass. Yet even as she relaxed, he continued rubbing, soothing away all memory of the pain.

He looked at her curiously in her burgundy Hoosier sweatpants and sweatshirt, and her dark hair she'd braided in one long braid. She touched it now, wondering what he thought of her without a sleeping *kapp*.

"Better now?"

She nodded and stretched out her leg. "*Mmm*, yes." She

gathered her sleeping bag and pulled it to her chest as if that would protect her. As if it was a shield, hiding the pounding of her heart.

The moonlight flowed around him, and his hair stuck up in all directions.

"I'm sorry I woke you." Her voice was no more than a whisper.

"I thought you were getting eaten by a bear."

She cocked her head. "You would have fought a bear to save me?"

"Of course. It would have been quite the story to tell."

She chuckled. Even though the dim light made it hard to see the humor in his gaze, she could hear it in his voice.

She'd been dreaming that she'd been running through these woods, trying to get to Portland. For the last year she'd been anxious about getting to school. She couldn't wait to finish her online classes and just start. But in her dream she'd been running *from* something, not *to* something. She'd been running away from the realization that her feelings for Caleb were growing. It was the very reason why she'd distanced herself from so many at home.

"I better get back to my tent. I don't want anyone to get the wrong idea."

"*Ja, danki.*" She waited for him to exit, and then zipped her tent closed. She couldn't think of many Amish men who would have done that—come running toward what they thought was a bear. Caleb was brave in so many ways.

Rebecca snuggled back into her sleeping bag, wondering what tomorrow would bring and trying to imagine that moment when she got on the train in Whitefish and headed to Portland for good. A twinge struck her heart; in a way it made her sadder thinking of that than when she'd left Indiana. Of course, most of her new friends didn't know the truth. Maybe once she told them, they'd be happy to see her go for good.

She hated deceiving them. If her decisions put a wedge between an established friendship—like hers and Marianna's— what hope did she have of these days turning into anything more than just a sweet memory? Some people were just in your life for a season. She'd have to think of this trip as just that: a fun time that filled in the days between her transition. Hoping they could be anything more would just hurt her heart . . . and could lead to hurts on the other side too.

CHAPTER

13

Caleb opened his eyes, wondering if he had dreamed that Rebecca had been crying out in the night. He lay there a minute remembering how she'd gotten a charley horse and remembering how he'd rubbed her leg. Growing up, his sister closest to his age, Bethany, had often had the same problem, and he'd learned to rub her leg just to keep her quiet. He must have still been half asleep to have been brave enough to rub Rebecca's leg like that. Thankfully, she'd been wearing sweatpants, most likely because she was afraid of getting cold in Montana.

He turned over and let out a low moan. Lying next to his pillow was a stack of the letters from his mem. Amos still slept—or at least he pretended to. Why didn't his friend get the hint? He didn't want to think about what was happening in Indiana. He didn't want to feel the guilt over what he'd left behind. *Who* he'd left behind.

Caleb picked them up, preparing to toss them into his duffel bag, when he noticed the second envelope from the top was open. He sat up in the tent and turned it over in his hands. Who had opened it . . . and why?

On the back was a note written in Amos' scribble: *I'm sorry. I thought this was a letter from my mem until I opened and started to read. You might want to read it.*

Caleb blew out a breath. He wanted to knock Amos on the side of the head. Instead he pulled out the letter and began to read.

Dear Caleb,

You haven't written home lately, and the phone number you gave me to leave a message on just rings and rings, but there is no answering machine that ever picks up. I thought if you had read last week's letter, you would have called home. There was someone who would have loved to talk to you on his birthday. Well, he couldn't have talked, but at least he would have listened.

Your dat is happy about the size of the crops. Harvest is going well, and the abundance has been a blessing from the Lord. We had the Schrock boys come over to help, and at the end they only accepted half of what Dat had been preparing to pay them. They said that he's helped their family so many times. Yet another blessing.

I was cleaning out your opa's trunk, and you won't believe what I found. There was a letter addressed to you! He wrote it just a few weeks before his stroke. I'm not sure why he never gave it to you. I think it would help you now. I have no doubt that you didn't just go to Montana to hunt. I suspect that you went to think about your own future and what you want from it. Or maybe who you want.

As you will see, the letter just stops abruptly. I'm not sure if there is more to it around here, maybe still inside the notebook he wrote it in? Or maybe he just got interrupted. If it's inside a notebook, I might find it. I bet it's around here somewhere yet. Your grandfather always was

124

a collector. There are piles of magazines, notebooks, and manuals that I'm still going through. Why he collected manuals for cars and microwaves and DVD players, I'll never know, except for the fact he liked understanding how the world worked.

Your sisters tell me to send you a greeting from them. They wonder if you'll be home for Christmas. I hope so. Anyway, I hope you find some peace in your grandfather's letter. It helps me to know that he'd come to peace with much he'd been discontent about.

Love, Mem

He turned to the letter from his *opa* next.

Dear Caleb, my namesake—

I never had a son, but I want you to know that having you as a grandson made up for it. You're my fishing buddy and my partner in crime. (You never did confess to your grandmother that we were the ones who broke her favorite flowerpot, did you?) I am proud of you in so many ways, but as I've been thinking of myself lately I'm not always proud of how I've been or how I've acted.

I haven't wronged you in any way, son, but maybe my words have. You see, it was easy to talk to you. To tell you all the areas I felt my life was lacking. I didn't hold back when I told you that I wished I'd made it up to bear hunt in Canada. Or that I would have liked to try to swim in the ocean just once. Remember that time we figured out how long it would take to drive my buggy to New York City? What a poor Amishman I've been at times . . . tending my fields when my mind was off exploring a different land.

I think to tell you this now, because I've seen the same look in your eyes. The look of wondering where you'd end up if you followed the sun into the horizon. The look that's there when a motorcycle drives by. I always thought I was doing my rightful duty to my church by not acting on my longings. But what I see now is that because of them, I haven't appreciated everything else that I hold in my grasp.

Yer oma and I were married forty-seven years before her passing, and I miss her more each day. I wish now I'd been a better husband more than I ever wished for another thing. Does that make sense, son? Don't look past love for adventure, as wonderful as I've made it up to be. Love is worth giving everything for. I know a great example of this—

The letter ended there, and if Caleb hadn't recognized his grandfather's handwriting, he never would have believed these words could be his. *Oma*'s death had been hard on his grandfather. What had he been going to say next? Was he going to urge Caleb to find a good woman and settle down? Caleb had a feeling he was.

"Maybe Mem put him up to it," Caleb mumbled under his breath. If his mother had her mind set on anything, it was him settling down, finding a *fraa*, and having a son of his own. Caleb returned the letter to the stack and lay back down, scratching his head. Would Mem approve of Rebecca? *Ja*, she would. At least until she saw the wandering in her eyes too. Wandering that matched his own. He just wished he had the guts to ask Rebecca about it. He'd noticed how nervous she'd seemed last night when Ike mentioned her family in Indiana. Why had she left? What did her leaving mean? Had there been someone else? A suitor?

Caleb's head hurt too much thinking about all of that. The best thing to do was to get up, get going. Movement took his mind off all the things that weighed on his heart. He'd start the fire if Ike hadn't already, check on the horses, and check on Rebecca too. That was the part he was most looking forward to. Maybe today he'd get more answers. Maybe today she'd start to take down the wall she'd so carefully built around her heart.

CHAPTER

14

Rebecca hadn't been able to sleep much after she'd woken up in the night. She'd drifted in and out of sleep, remembering how it felt to have Caleb there, coming to her rescue . . . even if it was a charley horse that she battled instead of a bear.

As soon as the first ray of morning light hit the tent, she'd been up, washed up at the creek the best she could, and dressed back in her Amish clothes and *kapp*. She was thankful for the coat that Millie had brought and wore it as she sat in front of the cold fire pit. She could see her breath as she exhaled and hoped the day was going to warm up. That was something she hadn't thought about when she'd made the decision to come on the trip. When one was cold, there wasn't a warm quilt to snuggle under by the woodstove. There wasn't a way to draw a hot bath either.

Rebecca took one of the sticks that they'd cut to roast marshmallows and used it to write in the dirt around the fire pit. C-A-L-E—

Footsteps sounded from behind her, and she quickly brushed away the letters with a swipe of her shoe. She turned to see Caleb striding toward her.

"Hi." His voice was still scratchy from sleep.

"Hi." She smiled. "Just wake up?"

Caleb scratched his head and brushed down his hair. "That noticeable?"

She pointed to his shirt and the puckered hole in the front. She'd like to think he'd dressed quickly so he could hurry out of the tent to see her. "Missed a button."

He glanced down and then a smile tilted up the left corner of his lips. "*Ja*, well, growing up with all sisters, you'd think I would have learned how to dress myself." He plopped onto the cold ground and lounged back against the log.

Rebecca shook her head. Any other Amishman would be taking down the tents or gathering more wood for the morning's fire. The Amishmen in Indiana worked from the moment they rose until bedtime. Unlike them, Caleb played as hard as he worked. And even more unnerving was the way he lounged on his side, fiddled with a stick, and then lifted his eyes to hers. "Have you been up long?"

"Long enough to wish I had a hot cup of coffee and maybe a book to read." She rubbed her hands together and hoped he'd get the hint about starting the fire and some coffee.

"My grandpa's favorite thing to read was *National Geographic* magazines. He read them as religiously as he read the *Budget*. He borrowed them from the neighbor—seemed to bring a new one home every time he went over to use the phone. Did you know that Montana is one place where they've found the most dinosaur fossils—over on the other side of the Rockies where all the big ranches are? *Opa* always talked about that. I wish he would have had a chance to go there. I'm pretty sure he never left Ohio his whole life, though he was probably one of the most traveled of Amishmen through the pages of a magazine."

"I didn't know that about Montana. In fact, I don't know

much about Montana at all. I hadn't even been planning on coming here until I was on the train." She folded her hands on her lap and dared to say the next words. "In fact, I was headed someplace completely different. Someplace that might surprise a lot of people, especially my family." She looked at him then, waiting for him to ask. She'd decided this morning that today was the day to confess about nursing school.

Caleb nodded, but his eyes were fixed on the tops of the trees. She followed his gaze. An eagle glided on the breeze, rising and lowering in a lazy circle.

"Montana is great. Often when I'm turning a bend in the road or coming to the top of a rise, I picture my *opa* at my side. I try to think what he'd point out first and what he'd say. Like that eagle. He'd probably talk about how he always wished he could go up in an airplane just once."

Rebecca pressed her lips together, wondering if Caleb was purposefully trying to ignore her. Didn't he care about her plans? It seemed like he was always interested in talking about everything except the things that mattered most to her heart.

Maybe I'm making more of our friendship than I should. Maybe Caleb doesn't see me any differently than his buddy Amos.

"Doesn't seem like much of an Amishman to want to go up in an airplane," she found herself saying.

He glanced over, his brow furrowed. "*Vell*, it doesn't mean he acted on it. Doesn't mean he didn't serve his community and church every day of his life. Isn't that what matters?" The anger in his voice wasn't hard to miss.

Rebecca shrugged. "It's just that most Amish people I know don't even think about those things. They don't think about flying or leaving their community or going to college. Do you ever think about that?"

"I came to Montana, didn't I?" He rose and kicked around

the logs from the fire pit as if trying to decide if he wanted to light it. "I get excited about climbing the biggest tree or bringing in the biggest buck. That doesn't mean I'm any less of an Amishman."

She blew out a breath of frustration. Why did he always have to turn everything back to himself? Was he that thick-headed not to realize that she wanted to share something important with him?

She was about to answer him when she realized his eyes were fixed on something behind her. She turned. Ike and Annie trudged down the road. They walked side by side, but it was clear from Annie's expression that she was not happy.

From the first time Rebecca had seen Annie, the owner of the West Kootenai Kraft and Grocery, it had been clear how much the woman was loved and respected in her community. Even though Annie was *Englisch*, she was friends with both Amish and *Englisch*. Annie was the designated cook for the trip, which Rebecca was thankful for. Rebecca knew a lot about baking and could cook a decent meal, but not under these conditions. Not over an open flame. Her stomach growled just thinking of the promised pancakes. She just hoped that whatever had happened between them would not hinder that.

They approached and said a quick good morning, then Annie sat despondently, staring off. She stretched out her legs and pressed down the wrinkles in her jeans as if doing so would also press the worries out of her mind.

Ike hunched down like a cowboy before the campfire, but there was no fire. As if realizing that, he sighed, and then rose and turned.

"I'll go get some firewood," he said to no one in particular.

Rebecca looked to Caleb, and he shrugged. She tried to think of something—anything—to say.

Caleb cocked one eyebrow and then rose. "If you'll excuse me, I'm going to go wake up Amos and then check on the horses. If my guess is right, I bet Millie is already in the meadow sweet-talking them and preparing them for the day's journey."

"Hurry back," Rebecca called, more for the sake of saying something—not that she needed anything in particular.

Annie stopped pressing on her jeans and instead turned her attention to her long blond ponytail, twisting it around her finger. Finally, Rebecca couldn't stand the awkward silence any longer.

"Is everything okay?"

Annie turned to her, surprised, as if she'd been so lost in her thoughts that she'd forgotten Rebecca was there.

"Oh, Ike . . . he makes me so angry. He just asked me for a date—not just dinner at the restaurant, but a real date down in Eureka."

Rebecca wasn't surprised by the news. She'd seen the way Marianna's uncle Ike looked at Annie. He watched her even when she didn't realize it. He listened to her words, really listened.

"I think that's wonderful . . . although I know it must be strange, to have an Amishman care for you. Have you ever thought about becoming Amish, Annie? I've heard it has been done before."

"Oh yes, but, well . . . it seems silly to talk like this when we haven't even had a date yet, but Ike has been talking for a while about leaving the Amish. He says he knows he can love God without having to be Amish."

"*Ja.* I've heard Marianna say the same thing. She wrote to me about that even before she decided to leave the Amish to marry Ben." Rebecca scowled, thinking about that. She'd been raised her whole life knowing the Amish way was the way

God required. She never considered that she could leave and feel justified in doing so. Guilt trailed along with her whenever she wasn't wearing her Amish clothes and *kapp*—not that she would ever admit that to anyone.

"The thing is, I know what it will cost him—in his life and with his community."

"Don't you think that's his choice? I mean, if his care for you is greater—"

"It's not just that. Ike has no idea what it will cost me."

Rebecca turned, surprised by the woman's words.

"I can't see myself being Amish. I've known the freedom that comes from a relationship with Christ for too long. That means Ike will leave . . . But, well, if I allow myself to love Ike and we get married, that will mean he would be in the *Bann*. You've been Amish your whole life, Rebecca. You know the rules: no money passing between the hands of those who've left the church."

"That means if Ike left the Amish church—and if you were married—no Amish person would be able to buy from your store."

Annie nodded. "Yes, and that's what happened to the previous owners. They were Mennonite, but both had been born Amish and had been baptized into the church. When they bought the store, it had been thriving, but under their ownership the sales plummeted. The bishop even preached against them. You are right—no money can exchange hands with someone under the *Bann*."

Rebecca did know. It was a way to urge people to turn back to the right ways—the narrow road. To allow people to live in their sin was unacceptable.

"Robert and I were able to buy the store for a good price because the owner was about to lose it all."

"Robert?"

Annie's eyes widened, as if she couldn't believe she'd said his name. "He was my fiancé. I loved him like I had never loved anyone before." Annie cleared her throat. "Which is another reason that dating scares me." She lifted her gaze and focused on Rebecca's eyes. "I haven't told Ike this, but I'm afraid of loving again . . . afraid of giving my heart away, just to have it broken."

Rebecca nodded. What could she say? Part of her was scared of the same thing. Even as she was drawn to Caleb, she worried that caring for him would mean walking away from what she was called to do. She could almost hear her mem's comments about other young women who got swept away by a guy's affection. *"That girl's* ab im kopp—*off in the head—every time he looks at her!"*

"You need to tell him the truth," Rebecca finally said. "Tell him what has you worried so. If it's true love, it'll be worth the risk." Rebecca folded her hands on her lap, wishing she could force herself to do the same thing.

"Yeah, I really should do that." Annie rose and walked over to the plastic tub filled with pots and pans and pulled out a skillet. "More than that, I should pray about it. I've been doing a fine job at making sure Ike didn't get too close. The harder part is relinquishing how I think things should happen and opening my heart up to what God wants. How does that verse go? 'For I know the plans I have for you,' says the Lord. 'They are plans for good and not for disaster, to give you a future and a hope.' I know God was talking to the children of Israel, but I also know those words apply to us too. If God has a plan for me, shouldn't I try to seek Him to find it?"

Annie put the pan down on a log and looked in the direction Ike had gone, as if she expected to see God's plan posted on the trees for her to read.

"I suppose I never really thought of it that way . . . that God has a plan." Rebecca tried to remember if she'd ever heard that in church. Not really. She often heard what she had to do to make sure she followed the Amish way, but were God's plans different from that?

She tried to wrap her mind around how God could have a unique plan for each person, yet also a certain way for His followers to live.

"We try to figure everything out, control so much, don't we?" Annie placed her hands on her hips and turned to Rebecca. "Thank you so much for helping me, Rebecca." Annie winked. "I think you being here, reminding me to turn to the One who knows everything, was part of His plan too."

Rebecca smiled, even though she'd done little to help Annie. If anything, Annie's words had gotten her thinking.

"Sweetie, would you like to mix up the pancake batter?" Annie asked. "I have some filtered water there and the measuring cups and such."

"*Ja*, of course."

"And don't forget to add in the huckleberries. They are the best part."

CHAPTER

15

The first day's ride had been easy. The logging road had been used in recent years, and the ground had been hard and not very rocky. But today the road had narrowed. Stubborn thickets crowded in. They trailed the others, and more than once Caleb questioned if he'd missed a turn and they were still on the right trail.

"Do you think we'll make it as far as yesterday?" Rebecca asked.

He could hear tension in Rebecca's voice.

"Is the trail already wearing on you?"

"I'm just trying to make conversation, that's all."

The huckleberry pancakes had tasted good, but now they felt like a brick in his stomach. Rebecca had been quiet this morning—too quiet. She had looked at him curiously, as if she waited for him to say something, do something.

Instead they talked about their home states—hers Indiana and his Ohio. Things were more similar than different in their Amish communities, but that was to be expected. They might have minor differences, such as if reflectors were allowed on their buggies or if motors were allowed on lawn mowers, but at the core their beliefs were the same. Always the same.

Caleb heard a roaring sound and guessed that up ahead a stream squeezed between two mountains. Trying to get a view of the cascading water, he noticed Ike approaching on the extra horse. Caleb pulled back on the reins, slowing his team. Ike's face puckered in concern.

"Is it the roadway?" Caleb asked.

Ike's horse paused beside them. "The road's fine, but it's Annie. She woke up with an awful stomachache. We're going to pull off for a bit. Mille and Amos said they'd stay with us."

"*Ja*, that's fine. We can go ahead and set up the site."

"Do you think I should stay with the women?" Chills raced up Rebecca's arms. It seemed so intimate—too intimate—for her and Caleb to head out alone. Surely they wouldn't agree to that, would they?

"*Vell* . . ." Uncle Ike paused for a minute, considering. "We really need an experienced male driver for each wagon. The horses aren't easy to handle. And I'd love to say that you could ride with one of our wagons, but we're already loaded down." He sighed. "But if it's a problem—"

"No problem," Rebecca interrupted. "It's just that, uh, if the women needed someone to talk to . . ." What else could she say—that back east it would be considered improper for them to head out alone? Just looking around it was obvious they weren't back east.

"Are we all right in heading out alone, then?" Caleb asked.

"Yes, of course!" Her voice sounded too perky, even to her. She offered Ike a wave as he headed back up the trail, and then their own wagon started up again to the clopping of the horses' hooves on the rocky road. Caleb whistled a low tune.

Rebecca was silent, looking ahead to the high, straight-rising mountains. She didn't say anything.

"Do you know something I don't?"

Rebecca sighed. "Annie's sick, all right. She's lovesick."

"What do you mean?"

"You can't see it? The way she looks at Ike? But she's afraid of what he'll lose—what she'll lose—if they confess their care for each other."

"Isn't that what love is about—having to surrender more than you thought you ever would?"

She glanced over at him and wrinkled up her nose. "Aren't you romantic?"

"Hey, hey, don't judge me before I finish. I was going to say that even though there are things you have to give up, it's worth it from what you gain." Caleb cleared his throat. "Not that I know from experience. But that's the way it seems to me. At least my sisters sure seem happier."

They passed Ike's wagon and Millie and Amos next. Amos seemed none too happy to be riding along listening to the stories of a senior citizen rather than of a beautiful young woman like Rebecca. At least with Millie one didn't have to worry about saying the right thing, doing the right thing. One didn't have to worry about gauging each conversation.

A little ways past the other two wagons, they came upon the waterfall. It was just off to the side of the road. Caleb stopped the team and jumped down from the wagon. He turned to her.

"Want to see me jump from the top?" He pointed from the top of the waterfall to the little pool at the bottom. "I wonder if I can do a flip in the air on the way down."

Rebecca gasped. "Caleb, don't you dare!" She stood and looked down at him, her face a mix of fear and anger. "That pool's not deep enough for certain . . ."

He took a step toward the water while at the same time keeping his eyes fixed on hers. Her mouth opened, and her cheeks turned bright pink. And what was that in her eyes? Tears?

"Hey, hey, now. I was just joking. Someone would have to be crazy to do that."

She pressed her fists into her hips, knuckles white. "*Ja*, and don't you think that describes you perfectly?"

He reached a hand toward her, and she reluctantly took it. Her hand was shaking. She stepped down from the wagon and tried to pull away, but he clung tightly to her fingers.

"Listen, I really am sorry. I was just joking. I didn't realize you'd take it seriously."

"Joke about other things than breaking your neck, will you? It's all fun and games for you, Caleb, but if you do get hurt, think about everyone else. What would we do? How would we get help for you?"

He wanted to apologize again, but it wouldn't do any good. Instead he blew out a breath, released her hand, and moved to the waterfall. He found a large rock, big enough for two, and then sat. He thought about kicking off his boots and dipping his toes into the water, but his playful mood of a few minutes before was gone.

A minute later Rebecca joined him, sitting next to him on the rock. She picked up a handful of small pinecones and tossed them in, one at a time. As each one plopped into the water, it sank briefly and then rose to the top and was carried away.

Rebecca cleared her throat but still refused to turn to him. To look into his eyes. "Listen, I'm sorry I reacted that way. I think my fears are coming out."

"Fears?"

"*Ja*. I mean . . . aren't you afraid at all? Aren't you ever afraid? Here we are in the middle of nowhere. We don't have cell service, and there are wild animals, acts of nature . . . Anything could happen. We already have one sick person . . ."

"I thought you said that Annie was just lovesick."

"Well, it could be that, but what if it's something else?"

"Then I suppose we'll just have to trust God. It's not like we're out here all alone. I mean, don't we believe that He's always with us? Always watching out for us?"

"*Ja*, that's what we're supposed to believe, but it's easier just focusing on things we can control. Like our *kapp*s. Like our gardens. At least it's easier for me to make plans and stick to them rather than letting myself lose my grip and just trust that everything will turn out in the end."

Rebecca picked up another handful of pinecones and started tossing again. "Millie said that when she looks at a pinecone she sees all the potential. She said there is the potential of a forest in each one. But for me . . . Well, I wish I could be like that. Instead I just consider how frail they are. And how easily they get carried away."

"But even if they get carried away, they can still land somewhere good, right? Just because they don't feel in control doesn't mean the potential isn't still there."

She glanced over at him. "Do you really believe that?"

He removed his hat and scratched, letting the sun warm the top of his head. "I've never really thought of that before, but I suppose I do."

"That's good, because I've never felt so out of control in all my life as I do on this trip. I can't help but be worried that you're going to do something crazy or that Marianna is going to have a problem with her pregnancy. At first it was exciting being out so far in the wilderness, but I'm ready to get back to civilization where things are safe."

He chuckled. "It's not like we're completely in the wilderness. There are roads here, Rebecca. It's not like we're off where no man has ever been before. And if Marianna needs help, it's only thirty minutes to Eureka, if you hurry."

She folded her arms over her chest. "You're not helping things."

"We should probably get going, then, get to the next campsite—closer to civilization. We have a lot to set up before the others join us."

They made their way back to the wagon and started out again. Within a few minutes they'd both settled in to the gentle rocking of the wagon as it moved back and forth.

"You know, I goof around, but I'm not going to put myself and others in harm's way. Contrary to popular opinion, I like living."

"That's good to know."

The breeze picked up, and it brushed against his face. To him, being in nature was better than being in a safe place. When people tried to order their world, that's what worried him. With order came rules and expectations—both of which he seemed to fail at repeatedly.

"I don't think you should worry about the trip," he said again. "It's something you'll never get to experience again. Relax, enjoy it."

"But what if something bad happens?" She bit her lower lip.

"Then we'll deal with it then. My *opa* used to tell me not to worry about thunderstorms and miss out on a sunny day."

"Funny, because my *oma*'s motto was to try to always be prepared."

He shrugged. "Then maybe—for the rest of the journey— we can find a happy medium between the two?"

Rebecca nodded. "*Ja*, I'd like that."

They journeyed on for another hour before they came to the campsite that Ike had described. It was a flat area before a tall rise. On one side there was a creek, and on the other side a large meadow perfect for grazing horses. The only thing that troubled him was the steep incline of the road. Ike had scoped the roads on horseback. Had he taken into account how hard it would be for the horses to pull a loaded wagon bed up to the top of the hill?

"What do you think? Should I try to park it up on the top or down here?"

A little smile brightened her face. "You're asking me? This is the first time in years that I've been away from cell phone service. I'm not really an outdoor person, and if I were to ever look for a campsite, I'd look for one with a bakery nearby." Rebecca chuckled and tapped her chin with her finger. "But . . . if you park at the top of the hill, we have a head start tomorrow. Also, it'll leave room for the other two wagons down here."

"Great idea. Pray, pray hard that we can make it to the top of that rise without any trouble."

The horses eased onto the sloping trail, pulling slow but steady. The wagon canted slightly.

Caleb glanced over at her, smirking. "This is steeper than it looks."

Just then the wagon jolted as the wheel hit a rock. Caleb's smile faded as he heard the splinter of overweighted spokes. The wagon dropped like a stone in a pond.

"No, no!"

A haunted look came into Rebecca's eyes, and she leaned toward him to keep from tumbling out.

"Climb over me and jump down, Rebecca!" Caleb said in her ear. "I don't think it's going to tip, but I don't want you to be in the way if it does!"

Rebecca didn't have to be told twice. She scrambled over him and jumped to the ground.

"Unhitch the horses!" he called to her before he followed, also jumping down to the ground.

Rebecca understood. If the wagon continued to tip, both the double tree and the shaft would be broken.

Instead of running up to the front of the wagon to help her, Caleb ran to the back and began unloading the bins and barrels. He worked as one man, but did the job of two with speed and efficiency. Rebecca unhitched the horses and led them back down the hill toward the pasture area. They seemed surprised, but happy that they were free to graze.

She returned back up the hill and found that the back of the wagon was unloaded. Not only that, but Caleb had already stabilized the wagon with a log and removed the wheel.

Sweat beaded his brow, and she quickly hurried to the tote with the bottled water and pulled one out. She handed it to him. "This isn't cold, but it should help."

Caleb glanced up, surprised. "*Danki*. I appreciate that, Rebecca."

"It's just water." She shrugged and sat down beside him. She pointed to the wheel. "Is it bad?"

"The good news is that it's just cracked. The bad news is that I don't have any wood glue to fix it." He leaned forward and studied the wheel closer. "I think the best thing would be to create a new spoke, but that'll take some time . . . and skill."

"I think you can do it." She tried to stay upbeat.

He turned to her, and she focused on his eyes. "I mean, if you can build a house, you can make a spoke, right?"

Caleb sucked in a deep breath, and his chest expanded. His eyes brightened, too, and she smiled. "What do you need? I can help."

He eyed the wagon wheel and then glanced back at her. "A solid piece of wood and the ax. Although I'm not sure I can engineer it good enough to fit right. People spend years studying the trade, and—"

Rebecca held up a hand, halting his words. "You'll never know until you try. And if you can jump off a huge cliff, you can do this, Caleb. I believe in you."

Caleb stood and straightened his shoulders. "*Ja*, I'll try, Rebecca. For you I'll try anything."

Rebecca stayed by Caleb's side as he found a branch and began to shape it with the ax. It was slow work, and as time passed, her stomach began to rumble. What was taking the others so long? If she was hungry, Caleb had to be too.

Without telling him what she was doing, Rebecca went down the hill and found a good spot for a campfire, and then gathered wood and got it started. It had helped that she'd watched the others over the last day. She then opened a few cans of beans and cut up some sausages. It wasn't a fancy meal, but it smelled good. Unable to hide her smile, she took it up to Caleb.

His eyes brightened as he spotted her. She looked and saw that he almost had the spoke done. Pride radiated from his face, and his mouth dropped open when he saw the plate she offered.

"You made lunch?"

"*Vell*, seeing that it's almost suppertime, I'd call it dinner." Rebecca smiled. "But it's warm and smells *gut*."

"So you started a fire? Did you clear the area and—" He prepared to stand as if to check out her work, and she placed a hand on his shoulder and pushed him down. "Don't you worry. I'm not going to be starting any forest fires, if you're worried about that. I've been watching you and Ike and Amos. I did a good job, trust me."

He placed the spoke on the ground and then stretched a hand to her.

She handed him the tin bowl filled with beans and sausages and a spoon and sat down on the stump closest to him. "And speaking of a good job, look at you! Why, it looks as if it'll work."

"Looks can be deceiving." Caleb shrugged. "But it's a good attempt. I'm just hoping that Ike can help me the rest of the way." He took a few more bites of his meal. "Wow, this is good."

"Glad you think so. I hope I didn't mess up Annie's menu too much. I—" It was then she noticed his pants—the tear near his calf and the blood. "Did you hurt yourself?" She placed her bowl on the stump and hurried over to him. Without asking if she could help, she lifted up his pant leg and eyed his wound.

"Did the ax slip?" She knelt down next to him.

"*Ja.* I learned right quick not to try to whittle down the wood by cutting toward me."

Rebecca studied the gash. It was at least four inches long, but she was thankful that it wasn't as deep as expected. "Hold on." She moved to her suitcase and pulled out her first-aid kit, then rushed back to him.

"You . . . have a first-aid kit with you?"

"This is no ordinary first-aid kit." She pulled out some gauze strips, some rubbing alcohol, and bandages. "Can you hand me that?" She pointed to his water bottle.

She rolled up his pant leg and then used the water in the bottle to clean the wound. She then got the alcohol and cleaned it again. Caleb winced slightly, but she paid him no mind. When everything looked clean, she placed gauze strips over the wound and then wrapped a bandage around it.

It was only when she was done that she glanced up at Caleb.

He seemed impressed. "*Vell,* I didn't know we were bringing a nurse on this trip. How handy."

"I'm not a nurse." Heat rose to her cheeks. "I—I just like to pretend." She should say more, she should at least mention the EMT classes she'd attended, but the words wouldn't form on her lips.

What would Caleb think?

She took a step back and then repacked her first-aid kit. She didn't want Caleb to know. Her chest grew tight, and it hurt just thinking about the disappointment in Caleb's gaze when he discovered her plans for her life didn't line up with their *Ordnung*.

Tell him, Rebecca. Tell him.

She opened her mouth, but Caleb stood and pointed down the hill. "Look, here they come!"

The two wagons pulled in and parked, and Ike hurried up the hill.

"Is everything all right?" Ike asked.

"It is now." Caleb stood. "It's steeper than it looks. I suppose I should have waited until you got here to help guide me up."

"You do have the heaviest wagon . . ." Ike eyed the pile of the wagon's contents on the side of the road. "But it seems as if you have a plan for how to fix the wheel." He looked at the spoke that Caleb had been working on.

"A plan, and someone by my side who's done a great job helping me." Caleb glanced at Rebecca. "I couldn't have done this without her." He winked. "Let's just say she passed with flying colors in my book."

CHAPTER
16

Annie was feeling better by the time they arrived. Rebecca watched her, wondering if she was still worried about her decision of whether or not to open her heart to Ike, but Annie went about preparing dinner for the rest of them as if she didn't have a care in the world.

Rebecca approached her as she peeled potatoes, cutting the peels so they fell into a plastic bag.

"I hope you don't mind that we got into the food," Rebecca said.

"No, not at all. I was hoping you would. I'm sorry things took longer than we thought they would. I headed into the woods because I thought I was going to be sick, and Ike was worried. He followed me, and . . . well, we had a good chance to talk."

"You did? That's wonderful. What did you decide?"

"We decided that it was okay to stay friends. I love the store, and he is not ready to leave the Amish. There's nothing wrong with just being friends, right?" Annie forced a smile, but Rebecca noted the pain in her eyes. Her cheerfulness was just a show. Rebecca guessed that deep down, Annie's heart ached.

"That's unacceptable." Rebecca crossed her arms over her chest. "Love matters more than those things. You do love Ike, don't you, Annie?"

Annie took in a large breath. Her eyes closed, then popped open again. "I suppose I do. But promise me . . ." She hurriedly continued, "Promise me that you'll just allow things to happen as they should. Pushing for one's way never works. I've lived enough days on earth to know that for certain."

Rebecca was thankful that Caleb had not shared about his wound or the fact that she'd bandaged him up. Maybe he was embarrassed. She guessed that to be true.

With the help of Ike, they used Caleb's handmade spoke to fix the wheel.

"It's not a long-term fix, but it should get us to Libby," Ike commented. "I'm impressed, Caleb." He patted Caleb's shoulder. "You did some fine work here."

After dinner they set up their tents, and then they gathered around the fire pit. As soon as the fire was crackling, Millie cleared her throat. Rebecca could tell from the look in her eyes that she had a story.

"We're heading to Kootenai Falls, and this area—all that we're passing through—used to be the home of the Kootenai tribe. They once lived east of the Rocky Mountains, over on the plains, but they moved here. Can you imagine living this way all the time? Feeling one with nature and living off the land?" Millie spoke with excitement, and her eyes widened as if she pictured herself there. Rebecca could picture it too. Millie would be the elder of the camp, passing down the history and stories from her people.

"My mother grew up in Libby," Millie continued. "One of my favorite places was the swinging bridge. In fact, it was on that bridge that Donald gave me my first kiss." She blushed. "Mother also told me if you crossed over the river and waited until dark, you could hear the Native American ancestors whispering. I don't know about that, but the falls were a holy place to them, and I get the same feeling. It's as if God created a special place for us to go, to remind us that He is near. That He will do beautiful things in our times, just as He did in theirs."

Rebecca liked listening to Millie's stories, and it made her think of what she and Caleb had talked about earlier. Did God have good plans—beautiful things—designed for each person even when one felt as if she was being carried away with life?

The warmth of the fire and the peaceful night caused her to grow sleepy. She rose to say good night, but Amos motioned for her to sit. She sat back down.

"Wait," he said. "You can't go anywhere yet. You don't want to miss this."

He rose and hurried to their tent, then returned with something in his hand. With a flourish he opened his pack and presented something to Caleb.

A small harmonica glimmered in the light of the campfire. Caleb took it. He shyly, briefly glanced over at Rebecca. "I don't know how to play too many songs. I do have a few favorites."

"Play for us, please," she said. "It seems like the perfect end to a wonderful day."

Caleb started with one of the hymns from the *Ausbund* that she knew well. The tune was slow, but there were strings of hope in the melody.

While most Amish didn't understand the words they sang in German, Rebecca's *oma* had worked to write down the translations for her after each service. She'd often said there was no use singing words one couldn't understand. As Caleb started a new chorus, Rebecca opened her mouth to sing along—not in German, but English.

> *The one who is not faithful in the smallest thing,*
> *and who still seeks his own good which his heart desires—*
> *how can he be trusted with a charge over heavenly things?*
> *Let us keep our eyes on love!*

Rebecca looked to Annie as she sang those words, but Annie quickly looked away. Rebecca wanted to look to Caleb, to let him see the care in her gaze, but letting herself get caught up in that gave her the same uneasiness as when she tossed a pinecone into the stream. Instead she kicked her shoe in the dirt on the ground and looked at her feet. Who was she to trail after love when there were so many needs? No, she needed to focus on nursing school first.

Their Amish ancestors had been imprisoned for their faith—for believing that one could have a personal relationship with God and could choose baptism as a personal step of faith instead of simply accepting infant baptism. Many of the first believers died in the dungeons of Passau, Germany—as they had learned in school—but their beliefs had lived on. Butterflies danced in her stomach thinking about that.

She considered how some losses actually fueled the desires and the beliefs in those left behind. Claudia's death had done that for her. It was true she never wanted to be in that position of weakness again, but, equally as true, she wanted to make sure that when she left the earth, she had succeeded at living a life that mattered. And, to her, nursing—caring for people and tending to their wounds—symbolized that.

When Caleb finished one song, he started in on another.

Rebecca stared into the night sky, certain the stars had never been so bright or had appeared so close. She looked to Millie and understood even more how important it was to feel connected with the land one lived on. Rebecca hadn't felt that in a while. Would she ever feel it again? But either way it was a problem. If she were to give in—to surrender to the feelings of her heart—it would ruin everything.

Caleb's face glowed as he played the harmonica. She couldn't read his mind, but she could take a good guess at what he was thinking. He felt a part of these woods. He wasn't one to live in a place like Portland that was filled with roads and cars and people who thought nature was the city park at the end of their subdivision. To open her heart to him would force him to choose. She couldn't do that.

Caleb played on, and one by one the others rose and went to bed. And in that moment she liked to think that this whole trip had just been about the two of them. And the songs he played now were for her.

After another few hymns, Caleb put his harmonica on the log and turned to her. "I wanted to thank you again for all that you did to help me. To care for me."

Rebecca pulled Millie's jacket tighter around her. "It wasn't anything special. Everyone else here would have done the same."

"They might have tried, but you had all the supplies you needed. You had the skill."

She nodded. She was tired—her whole body seemed weary—but she'd never have been able to sleep knowing that Caleb was sitting less than ten feet beyond her tent. And even though she worried about the questions he would ask, she remained.

"It's a beautiful night. It reminds me of ones back in Ohio

when some of my friends would be at the Youth Singings and then sneak behind the barn to kiss the girls."

"*Ach, ja*, and it was your friends and not you?" She forced a chuckle even though her heart felt heavy, oh, so heavy.

"*Vell*, I didn't say that. Don't all Amish boys do things that would make their mems blush?" He fiddled with the harmonica and then slipped it into the pocket of the flannel shirt that he wore over his Amish shirt and suspenders.

"So have you kissed many girls?" Her eyes widened with interest as she asked him. She couldn't see his full face, only the lighted part that faced the moon, but he was handsome.

He winked at her. "A few. I forced myself to."

"*Ja*, I imagine."

"It's partly the truth. All my friends were starting to date. I felt there was something wrong with me for not spending all my time watching the young women and trying to pick a bride. I went on some dates and kissed a few girls hoping to feel something. The kisses were nice . . . but I couldn't think of a life with them past that. Every other Amishman on the planet wants a *fraa* who can cook well and tend to a house, but I'd like one with a twinkle of adventure in her eye."

"Like someone who'd join a wagon ride with strangers she didn't know?"

"Exactly."

"Caleb, that was just a joke."

"Not to me it wasn't."

He reached over and placed his index finger under her chin, and then raised it slowly so their eyes could meet. She saw something there. Something that wasn't expected. Something in his gaze that the Amish hymns had brought out: loneliness.

She didn't want to tell him that she'd felt the same loneliness. Yet while he'd tried to find affection in his past, sought it in being with her, she'd pushed it away. There was an ache inside, knowing that she was doing the very thing she'd promised herself she'd never do until after her schooling was complete. She allowed someone to enter into the tall walls of protection she'd placed around herself.

He's going to hate me when he finds out that our care for each other can't go any further than it has—that I've already chosen a different path.

She pulled her head back and looked away. His hand dropped to his side.

"You know that you can tell me anything, don't you?" His words were low, soft, so that no one in the nearby tents could hear them.

"*Ne* . . . no, I can't." She stood and took a step back toward her tent. "I've made some choices, about my future. As much as I want to get to know you better, it's not possible. I'm thinking that tomorrow I should ride with Millie and Annie."

The smile on Caleb's face faded, and he mumbled something under his breath.

"What was that?"

He stood too. "I said, 'Does she think I'm going to give up this easy?'"

"I'm not worthy of you, Caleb. I'm not what you're looking for. I guarantee that—"

"Don't you ever say that again. You have no idea."

She turned her head. "I'm not as brave as you think I am. I'm just running, that's all. I've hurt so many people, and I don't even feel guilty about it."

"You haven't hurt me, and I think others will offer you more grace than you think if you give yourself permission to let them in."

She focused on the fading fire.

"The friendship we've developed over the last few days is too good to just ignore," he said.

"And what about my running?"

"Yes, what about that? Are you going to get to the place where you trust me enough to tell me what that's all about? I have a feeling I know."

She paused then and tilted her chin. "Oh, you do, do you?"

"Well, I don't know exactly, but I'm smart enough to know what pieces about you don't fit. What you did today, bandaging up my leg . . . Well, that wasn't just an ordinary bandaging job. It's like you're a nurse or something, disguising yourself under an Amish *kapp*."

"How do you know that's not the truth?" She chuckled, trying to keep things light, but deep in her gut a knife twisted. How could she have been so foolish to reveal so much to him with her actions? "I'm not a nurse, but there's . . . Well, there's a story behind that. There is a reason why I take it so seriously. There is a reason why I get so bothered and worried when someone's doing something dangerous."

"Can you tell me about it, Rebecca?" Caleb leaned in closer to her, and his face was lit by the warm, orange glow from the campfire.

Her chest felt tight and thick, and she blew out a heavy breath, wishing her tension would rise like the smoke from the fire and disappear. Instead it clung to her. She had to do it. She had to tell him the truth. If she cared for Caleb, she had to take a risk.

She returned to the log she'd been sitting on. The smoke from the dying fire hurt her eyes. She rubbed them, and she hoped Caleb didn't think she was crying. There would be time enough for tears. They were always there—closer than she ever wanted them.

Caleb sat beside her and waited for her to pull her heart from her chest, turn it over in her hands, and spill it.

"I've wanted to be a nurse for seven years," Rebecca finally said. "It'll be eight years on September 19."

"It wasn't something you've always wanted to do?"

Rebecca shook her head. "Never thought of it. Until that day . . . Since then I haven't thought of anything else."

The tears came after all, throwing her off guard.

He sat. He waited. His blue eyes narrowed into slits as he concentrated on her breaths, waiting for her words. Rebecca tilted her head. His compassion surprised her, even though she didn't know why. There was nothing expected about this man.

She turned her head sharply to the side and stared at the forest of trees that looked like every other forest of trees they'd driven past. He cleared his throat, but she refused to look at him.

"Did you lose someone, Rebecca?"

She nodded and then closed her eyes, trapping the tears.

"She was my best friend." The words caught. "Well, my sister . . . but even more than that, my friend. I—I don't think I can talk about it."

"Okay, you don't need to."

She expected him to prod but was thankful he didn't. She felt his hand on her shoulder. No matter how she tried to hold them back, the memories resurfaced whether she was ready for them or not.

She'd never wanted to talk about it before—not with anyone. But for some reason it felt right, natural, for Rebecca to open her heart now. What would he think if she dared to share her story?

CHAPTER

17

Even though she was sitting by the campfire, in the middle of the Montana woods, her thoughts took her back again. They were always willing to take her back, no matter how much her heart ached in doing so.

It was her youngest sister, Misti, who had been first to warn them of the problem. "Something's wrong with Claudia! Come quick!" Rebecca had tossed down the shirt she'd been folding and rushed to the door. Since Claudia was getting close to the time of the *boppli*, she'd been staying next door at their *aenti*'s house. While Rebecca's family home was still full of younger kids, *Aenti* Diana had two empty rooms.

"We found Claudia on the floor curled in a ball," Rebecca told Caleb. "The pains had come on all fast-like, and my mem told her not to worry. She and my aunts always had their babies fast."

The memories were there, as fresh as if it had happened yesterday.

"We got Claudia to her feet," she said, "and Mem sent Misti next door to call for our driver."

Rebecca let out a long sigh. "I wonder now if everything

would be different if we would have called for the ambulance right then. Of course there is no way we could have known . . .

"Fifteen minutes later the driver still hadn't arrived, and Claudia told us she had to push. Even Mem was surprised, but she'd birthed eight children herself, and she had worked assisting a midwife when she was younger.

"Mem told Claudia that we'd deliver that *boppli*, and by *we* I knew she meant *me* too. Mem directed orders as if she'd been doing it all her life. Ten minutes later Claude slipped into this world. He was a huge baby—over nine pounds. And ten minutes after that Claudia slipped from this life into the next."

"What happened?"

"She started hemorrhaging. Mem didn't know how to stop it. I didn't know how either. I wish . . . My one regret in life is that I wish I would have known how to stop her bleeding. Mem was panicked too. She'd never experienced that before. I stood there watching my sister's life slip away, and I felt helpless. If I'd only had the right education . . ." Her words caught, then she continued. "Misti ran back to call for the ambulance then, but by the time they arrived, there was nothing they could do."

"And you saw it all?"

"I stood there and held my sister's hand. I was helpless. I never felt so useless. I kept telling her about her son, hoping that would make her fight for her life. But what good did that do? She was gone. Gone just like that."

Rebecca felt tired now. Weary from telling her story.

"I'm sorry you had to face that, Rebecca."

She glanced over at Caleb, and she could tell he wanted to say more. But what? What could someone say to ease her pain?

"I'm working on my nursing degree," she finally said. "I'm working to be prepared. Maybe that helps you understand a little more about me now."

Caleb nodded, and she rose and bid him a quick good night. People always felt uncomfortable when she told them her story, and she understood why. No one ever liked to talk about death. It was easier to talk about anything else. But as she walked to her tent, Rebecca realized that just because one didn't like to talk about it didn't mean it wasn't going to happen. And no matter how much she prepared, one could never prepare enough—although she wished that wasn't so.

Caleb woke early, and he couldn't get Rebecca's story off his mind. For the last few months he'd been running from what she'd had no choice but to face: death. He didn't want to think about the hurt of not having his *opa* there to talk to, to lean on, but Rebecca had had no choice in losing her sister. She'd had no chance to say good-bye. Not really.

Caleb sat in the quiet of the morning and opened another letter from his mem. This one was from a few months prior.

Dear Caleb,

Sometimes we all forget that you're in Montana. More than once I've set the table and included a plate for you. I know, son, that you are facing the most pain after your grandfather's stroke—you two were so close—but the rest of us are trying to do the best we can too.

My best friend, Elizabeth, came to see me yesterday. She cared for her parents for many years when they were both ill and faced their loss. She's walked the path that we do now.

Elizabeth goes to a New Order church now where they do more preaching about things than we typically hear, and while I don't believe that I want to add any of their new ways into our way of living, she did say something that I haven't forgotten since.

Elizabeth told me, "We just think we are in the land of the living, and that we're going to die, but when we believe in God the opposite is true. We're in the land of the dying, and because of Jesus we're going to the land of the living. The land where there is no more pain, no more tears, and where we'll be with Christ for eternity."

I don't know why I'm supposed to write that today. Or why you're supposed to read it, but maybe—with whatever you're dealing with, son—it gives you hope. Opa lived a good, active life, and I don't think he would have any regrets.

If you were to live your life today without regrets, what would you be doing? Would you be where you are now—this day? I've been thinking of that, and I have to ask you too. For me the answer is yes. Many would think that an Amish woman doesn't live an exciting life, but it's a fulfilled one. I've been surrounded with piles of laundry, but also my children's and now grandchildren's laughter. I've served up many meals, but I've been served smiles and warm embraces in return. I live a life seeing the beauty of God in creation, and that changes me deep in my heart. It's not an exciting life, but it's a good one. I suppose it just takes me pausing to enjoy it. Opa's stroke has caused me to do that.

I hope everything is gut for you in Montana. We still haven't heard from you, although Amos wrote his mem and said you are doing well. We hear you are building houses. We read in the Budget that one of the Amish families up there opened their back door at night to let *in their dog and a bear cub came in instead. They didn't realize it until morning when the man of the house had his glasses on. Did you hear that? It's a good thing that the mother bear didn't come around.*

Your sister Miriam is due to have another boppli. I believe the little one will be born before you return, unless you surprise us. I wish the West Kootenai community was closer. I believe your dat would travel there if he didn't have so much farmwork. I know you understand. Also, danki for sending part of your paycheck. With it, Dat was able to buy a new horse. She's a beauty, and he named her Montana Sky. Sky for short.

If you can, please write and tell us what it is like there. Do you like the community? We miss you, son. The losses seem to pile up.

Love, Mem

Caleb couldn't remember the last time he'd cried, but the tears came now. Hot and fresh on his cheeks. He quickly wiped them away and then folded up Mem's letter and put it back into the envelope before homesickness overtook him.

He didn't know why he had waited so long to read Mem's letters. Then again, he did. Reading them would change things. It would make him think about life, about going on without *Opa*. But today, with Rebecca by his side, that suddenly didn't seem as daunting as it once had.

CHAPTER

18

Caleb had rushed through the chores at record speed. As Annie finished making breakfast, he packed up all the tents. When they washed up dishes in the creek, he gathered up the horses and hitched them to the wagons. Others watched him curiously, but they didn't ask him what his hurry was. It wasn't even nine o'clock when they were already on the road for the day. As he settled on the wagon seat, Caleb's heart nearly felt like it would burst with Rebecca by his side.

"Rebecca, I couldn't sleep last night. Mostly because I kept thinking about you. My mem has always called me impulsive. If I see a tree, I want to climb it. If I see a high cliff over the lake, I jump first and don't think about hitting the water until I'm midair. And after you told me about losing your sister, well, I've never felt so close to another person. It's got me thinking . . ." His words jumbled in his mind and he tried to sort them, tried not to act too excited about the realization he wanted her—needed her—in his life for longer than this trip.

Rebecca lifted a hand, interrupting him. "Caleb, wait. I need to tell you something."

"Don't you want to hear what I have to say?"

"I don't deserve to hear those words—any words of kindness."

He looked over at Rebecca. She was biting her lip. She wiggled from side to side, as if trying to get comfortable. And then she pressed her lips into a thin line, as if she was trying to keep her pent-up words from escaping.

"I don't know how to tell you this. I don't want to tell you, but I have to. I just have to make myself say it." Her words spouted out, causing his shoulders to tense.

"When I left Indiana, I did it with no plans to go back for a very long time. I snuck out and hitched a ride to the train station, and I packed my suitcase without Amish clothes."

"I don't understand." The road got bumpy, and Caleb knew he needed to do a better job at guiding the horses over the terrain—especially with the makeshift spoke—but all he could focus on was her words.

"Marianna urged me to tell you on the first day of our trip—to tell you that I don't have plans for returning to Indiana, for being Amish. I didn't even add any Amish clothes to my suitcase. I just happened to be wearing them when I left. The ones I've been wearing this week belong to Marianna, and the only reason I put them on in Montana was because I saw you at the lake. You impressed me, Caleb, and I wanted to get to know you better. I didn't think anything serious would *kumme* out of it, but I knew you wouldn't even look at me twice unless I was wearing Amish clothes.

"I lied, Caleb. I lied when you asked about my family. We're not close. I've been pushing them away."

He heard her words and he felt them, like small jabs to his heart. "Why—why are you leaving?"

"I want to go to nursing school. I already have my high

school diploma and my first year of college done. There are too many unnecessary deaths in my community. I never want to feel helpless again, like I felt when Claudia died. Yet . . . what I didn't realize is that on my quest to bring healing to people, all I've done is bring them pain. I've been hurting my parents, over and over, keeping them at arm's length. I've hurt my friends. And now . . . I know I've hurt you."

Caleb didn't know what to say. What to do. A flood of anger rushed over him. She'd been sitting by his side, wearing that *kapp* and dress, acting the part. His fists tightened around the reins. The nerves in his neck tightened until he was sure they were going to snap. "Does anyone else know?"

"Millie." Her voice was small, timid. "She asked me about it that day we went for huckleberries. She heard it from Susan Carash."

Caleb smacked his forehead. "If Susan knows, it's only a matter of time before the rest of the folks in West Kootenai know." His face felt hot. His shoulders tightened. He reached back and rubbed his neck. "So I'm the fool. I'm the one who's driving you and wooing you. I'm the laughingstock."

"Caleb, no." The words shot from her mouth. "I never meant for it to be like that."

He jerked his head and narrowed his gaze. "Oh, so you just put on the *kapp* and dress for fun? This is all one big joke, right, Rebecca?"

"Don't you understand? I don't want to leave the Amish. If I could become a nurse and get baptized into the church, I'd do it without question. I'd do it Sunday if they let me. It's not about that. More than anything, I don't want to ever face that feeling of helplessness again. Claudia died and I could do nothing about it. I felt so small, so weak. Ever since I've had the chance, I've done something about it."

"We Amish are *gut* at working," Caleb interrupted. "And it seems some of us are good at deception too."

"Caleb." Her words released in a breath. "I thought you of all people would understand. You just lost your *opa* . . ." Tears filled her eyes.

"Don't bring my *opa* into this." Caleb's words sounded like a hiss, even to his ears. "And don't think that you—one person—can make that big of a difference. We are not that important, Rebecca. We are not pinecones with potential forests inside us. And if we were truly Amish, we would accept death, accept sickness as it comes, instead of trying to fight it. You're not God," he spat. "And obviously wearing a *kapp* doesn't bring you any closer to being Him."

Rebecca didn't know why she'd hoped for anything different than the words Caleb had just told her. Similar words would come from her parents. She'd already dishonored them by hiding what she'd been doing. They'd had no idea she'd been taking college classes behind their backs. When they discovered it, they'd probably be happy she'd left. Happy they'd escaped the shame.

She'd also seen the distance her decision had put between her and Marianna. They had been the best of friends, and yet Marianna had almost seemed relieved when Rebecca chose to go on the wagon trip. Marianna was no longer Amish, but that hadn't changed her attitude, her heart. Perhaps there were some things nobler than a career to leave their Amish community for—love being at the top of the list. Or at least Marianna thought so.

But now she'd never know what that was like. She'd never have a chance to explore that possibility with Caleb.

The tears came, although she wished they wouldn't. She had no reason to cry. What Caleb had said was true. She wanted to tell him that she'd tried to confess the truth to him a few times, but it would do no good. They'd had hours sitting side by side. She'd had plenty of chances.

Rebecca turned her head and watched the scenery roll by, wishing she was anyplace but here. She wished she hadn't come. And the worst part was . . . the worst was not over. When her parents finally figured out where she was, she'd hear it all again. Rebecca nibbled on her lower lip. Should she just disappear for good? Become a nurse and not return to the Amish community? Take the money her *oma* had given her and start a new life somewhere else? She'd never be appreciated.

They rode in silence for the next few hours. They sat only a foot apart on the wagon bench, but it could have been miles for the coldness that passed between them. Rebecca had opened her heart—at least for a little while—and now she felt the wall going up again, brick by brick by brick.

Ike was all smiles when they arrived at the campsite for lunch. Caleb jumped down from the wagon and unhitched the horses so he could take them to the nearest watering hole.

"What has you so happy?" Caleb muttered under his breath as he strode by.

Ike removed his hat and brushed his hair back from his face. "Why, I'd have to say that I just spent two hours riding beside the most beautiful woman in Montana." Ike narrowed his gaze. "What got you so upset?"

"Me? The same." Caleb stomped off, angry at himself for not seeing Rebecca's deception. Angry at Millie, Ben, and Marianna, and everyone else for not saying something to him. For letting him look like a fool. He took his horses to a small creek and let them drink until they had their fill of water. He said nothing to Millie as she did the same.

"So, I guess you found out about nursing school?" Millie commented.

Caleb didn't think she deserved an answer to that. Instead he needed to find a way to get his anger out. Back at the lunch spot, he strode up to Amos. He pointed to a large, long log that had been cut in recent months and was lying on the side of the road, most likely to keep the road clear for logging trucks. "I bet I can throw that farther than you."

Amos tilted his hat back on his head. "I think that's a challenge."

Ike strode up. "Isn't anyone going to invite the old man to your competition?"

Caleb slapped him on the shoulder. "If you think your back can handle it."

Annie sidled up to Rebecca, handing her a ham sandwich. "I think someone's showing off."

"Not for me, he isn't." Rebecca wrapped the string from her *kapp* around her finger. "I don't believe Caleb cares what I think." She held the sandwich but had no desire to eat it. Her stomach felt tight. Her throat ached from swallowing down her emotion. Maybe she was coming down with something. Still, she took a bite under Annie's watchful eye.

"I think he cares too much." Annie sighed. "Guys just show it differently."

Rebecca watched as Ike put on work gloves. Then he rolled the log to the center of the dirt road and lifted it so it stood on end, holding it there. "Shows it like that?"

Ike then walked around it, still holding it, sizing it up. The log was taller than him.

Caleb and Amos walked down the dirt road. Annie, Rebecca and Millie stayed to the back of Ike, by the horses.

Chills traveled up Rebecca's arms. In her opinion, frustrated males, big logs, and throwing weren't going to amount to anything good. "They're not going to hurt themselves, are they?"

Annie pressed a finger to her lips. "Probably, but who can stop them?"

As Rebecca watched, there seemed to be some unspoken rules to their contest. The others watched approvingly as Ike squatted down, put his hands under the log and lifted it, leaned it against his shoulder, and took a few steps. The log swayed, and Ike scrambled to catch his footing.

Just as Rebecca was sure he was going to lose hold of it and have it crash down upon him, Ike grunted loudly and gave a big heave, tossing it forward. The log flew up, flipped, and its top end hit the ground. For a second Rebecca thought the log was going to flip forward toward Caleb and Amos. Instead it fell back toward Ike.

"Ohh . . ." A moan escaped from everyone's lips, and then it was Amos' turn. He went through the same ritual, and like Ike's toss, Amos' hit on end but then fell backward toward him.

Ike strode to them, his shoulders back and chest puffed forward. Annie offered him a bottle of water, and he took it, drinking half of it in one gulp.

"They call it the caber toss," Ike commented, approaching Rebecca.

"So it really is a sport?" Rebecca asked. "You're not just making it up?"

"No, miss." Ike wiped sweat from his brow. "We're not just making it up."

"I'm sorry, I didn't mean to sound disrespectful."

Ike took another step toward her. "*Ach*, you didn't. But this is a real thing. It's part of the Highland Games, and it's a way for a man to win his honor . . . or to use his muscles to ease an aching heart."

She touched her fingers to her lips, understanding what Ike was saying. Caleb had a few wounds that needed to be healed. Ones she had caused.

She watched as Caleb bent down and lifted the log. If she hadn't been looking so intently at his face, she would have missed the way he looked at her out of the corner of his eye for the briefest second. And then, sucking in a deep breath, Caleb took two steps and hoisted the log into the air. It flew higher than the others and landed on end. Rebecca found herself clapping, sure that it was going to topple over. Caleb was sure too. He lifted his hands high into the air and turned back to the others.

"See!" he called. "That's how you do it!"

The log teetered, but instead of falling forward, it fell back.

"Caleb, watch out!" Amos called.

Caleb glanced back and then jumped out of the way. Seconds later the log slammed down just where he'd been standing.

"He . . . he could have been killed." Rebecca's voice quivered. Her knees began to tremble and she hurried away from the others. The world around her turned to shades of gray, and she didn't know what to do. Her stomach rumbled and she placed a hand over the center of it, sure she was going to throw up. She moved toward the wagon and sat on top of the plastic bin that held their lunch items. Leaning over, she rested her elbows on her knees.

"Are you okay, sweetie?" It was Millie's voice.

"Yes, fine, just scared, that's all." She attempted to keep her voice from trembling. No matter how she tried, she couldn't stop the pain from swelling. She had the same feeling, deep in her gut, that she'd had when she lost Claudia.

"Sweetie, didn't you see? The log didn't hit him."

"Ye–yes. I know."

How could she tell Millie that it was so much more than that? Rebecca had thought she was making all the right decisions, but instead she felt as if all that she cared about was like sand sliding through her fingertips.

"I'm ready to just be there, Millie," she said with a big gulp. "I just want to be in Portland. I want to . . . I want to not hurt anyone else again. Or be hurt."

"Oh, darling." Millie sat beside her. "Don't we all wish that? If Johnson's 'No more tears' was for sale at the five-and-dime, such a thing would be all sold out by now." She took Rebecca's hand and squeezed. "But I know one thing: I know that God has a plan for you right here." Millie stamped her boot on the ground.

"How do you know that?"

"Because you're here . . . and I'm here too. God has put us both here for a reason."

She gazed up into the older woman's face. "I care for him, Millie."

"I know you do."

"But I can't. If I do, it'll ruin everything."

"Not the most important things." Millie smiled. "I know something else, Rebecca . . . if you'll allow me to say it."

Rebecca turned and looked at the older woman, focusing on her eyes. She waited, and then she breathed out a sigh. "What is it?"

"There will come a time when there will be no more pain. No more heartache. If we had it here, we wouldn't need eternity, and if we had no need for eternity, we'd have no need for Jesus. Following Him isn't just a set of rules, like so many think. But God's available to be here and to help us. All we have to do is pray—to ask for wisdom and to not let our own ego get in the way as we try to figure out everything on our own."

Even though her stomach still roiled, Rebecca felt a lightness in her chest from Millie's words. She'd been trying to tackle everything on her own for so long.

"You know, I had a sweet friend, Ida Mae, who passed away not too long ago," Millie said. "And she had a very special box. It was called a Promise Box. Every time she read God's Word and she came upon one of God's promises, she'd write down the promise on a piece of paper, fold it up, and put it in the box. She also wrote letters—just to herself—of things God was doing in her life. Every time she got discouraged, she'd go back to that box and read another promise . . . or she was reminded of a way God worked."

Rebecca nodded, thinking of how God had worked in her life. He'd given *Oma* faith in her dream. He'd provided finances for schooling. He'd provided her friend at the library to offer her a computer and help her with online classes. Even Lora had often given her rides and never requested payment.

"I liked her idea, but there's one I like even better: I heard this woman on the radio who said that after her mother died she found a similar type of box in her mother's bedroom. It was filled with prayers—for herself, for her children, and even for the needs of strangers. Every time a worry filled her mind, this woman would write it down, fold it up, and give it to God. From her worries over finding the right paint choice when painting the dining room walls to discovering she had cancer . . . all her needs went in there. And to her it was symbolic of turning the cares over to Him. So I started doing that. Do you want to see my God box?"

Rebecca's eyes widened. "You brought it with you?"

"Of course. Who am I to think that we were going to make it through this trip with no worries?" Millie patted Rebecca's knee and then rose. She went to the back of the wagon Amos had been driving and rifled through a red suitcase. A minute later she returned with a simple shoe box. She sat again and took off the cardboard lid. Inside, the box was half filled with little scraps of paper. Millie pulled one out and unfolded it.

"'Dear God, I pray that that sound my truck is making isn't anything serious,'" Rebecca read.

Millie nodded. "It was just my brakes. I got them squared away and it didn't cost too much."

Millie opened another one. *"'Dear God, please help Ellie Sommer learn to read better.'"* She refolded it. "I was talking to Ruth one day at the store and she said the teacher was worried. They got Ellie's eyes tested, and she doesn't have a problem with her vision, and I told Ruth I'd turn it over to God."

"Go ahead," she continued, "pick out a few."

Rebecca grabbed a couple of pieces of paper. She unfolded the first one. *"'Lord, please let Marianna's baby stick this time.'"* Rebecca offered a sad smile. "I hope this prayer does work, Millie."

Then she opened the next one. *"'Dear Lord, help Rebecca see how much You love her, and help her accept the love of others too.'"*

Millie's eyes widened, as if she was surprised that one—of all the pieces of paper—was the one Rebecca picked.

"Is that the way you see things, Millie?"

Millie shrugged. "It's not your fault, you know."

"What's not my fault?"

"Your sister's death. I know I'm old, but I have good hearing. I heard you telling Caleb last night."

Rebecca lowered her head. "It feels that way. Like I should have been able to do something to help her."

"Danger, death, is all around us, Rebecca. No matter how we prepare, we can't keep it at bay. Who knows? Today might be my last day on earth."

Rebecca gasped. "Don't say that, Millie."

"It's true, darling, and I've nothing to worry about. I've crossed the bridge."

"The bridge?"

"You better believe it. Now, school doesn't do much for me, but I do like to study my Bible. Did you know that the word for *priest* in Latin is *pontifex*, which means 'bridge builder'? Jesus is the bridge builder. He's the only One who can carry us from this world of sin and pain to God. Just like that big bridge over Lake Koocanusa, we can't get over to God's eternity on our own strength. I may be able to jump five feet across, and you ten feet, but neither is enough. Yet with the kiss from a friend and His willingness to be offered up, Jesus died once and for all, sacrificing Himself. And He not only will carry us across someday, but until then He wants to carry our concerns to His Father."

"The truth is, Millie, I'm afraid to pray. Because what if I do and God leads me a different direction than I had planned?"

"My pastor told me something once, and I've thought of it often—daily, almost. He said something like, 'If we were all-loving and all-knowing like God, we'd choose just as He does.' It makes sense, doesn't it?"

Rebecca gasped as Millie said those words. "I don't know about that. I wouldn't have chosen to have my sister die . . . no matter what."

"I wouldn't think you would, but somehow God allowed it. He had a purpose that you might never know. Maybe part of it was to put you on the path you're on. Maybe part of it was to introduce you to Caleb."

Rebecca placed her fingertips to her temples. It hurt her brain to think about those things. It hurt to think that she was going to have to face a lifetime of hurting.

"Do you think I could close my eyes for just a few minutes? Rest?" Rebecca pointed to a shady spot under a tree.

"Of course, darling. I'll wake you when we head out. Sometimes the best thing we can do with our minds and hearts is to allow ourselves to rest. After all, a heavy heart takes a lot of work to carry around."

CHAPTER

19

Caleb could see his breath on the morning air. There was even a chill on the ax handle as he lifted it, feeling its weight, wondering which weighed less—the ax or his heart.

Fall was usually his favorite time of year, but today the cold seemed too much. Even the idea that hunting season was one day closer did nothing to ease his frustration.

Annie emerged from her tent with their tin coffeepot. Had she known, too, that Rebecca was wearing Amish dress but had no plans to stay Amish? Had Millie said something? Were they offering silent pity for the way he'd been acting so stupid? He wished he could ask Annie, but that would only make things worse. If he talked about Rebecca, said too much, then they'd all figure out he'd had feelings for her . . . and then he'd really look like the fool.

The morning warmed up quickly, and Caleb was only partly surprised when Millie asked if she could ride with him that day. She walked with quickened steps with her stadium cushion tucked under her arm. He offered his hand, and Millie took it, climbing up into the wagon as if she were half her age. They hadn't been riding very long when Millie pulled off her cowboy hat, allowing the sun to warm the top of her head.

"Do you like stories?"

"Yes, of course. Especially ones from you, Millie." Was she going to repeat the same stories she'd already shared with Amos? Wouldn't surprise him.

"Good, because I have one to share. I started dating my husband when I was twenty-one years old. Kids always made a big deal of that birthday, but my mind wasn't on experiencing life with friends. Instead I focused it on one man. Every night I prayed for my future husband, and deep down I hoped it was Donald.

"Donald was on the football team at my small community college. I'd often see him wearing his jersey around campus. We didn't have a great team, and they hadn't won very many games, but Donald didn't seem to mind. I liked that about him. He was the type of person who would give his all no matter what he did.

"We were in one class together, and we were allowed to sit wherever we liked. Most people had their own seats, their territory. I found myself moving seat by seat by seat—one seat closer to him every class time. Soon he was just a row in front of me, and I tried to strike up a conversation. Finally, one day he looked at me and smiled. I later found out it was because I had ink on my cheek from my pen, but I didn't know it. I started talking about Shakespeare, which I knew he enjoyed because of some of the class discussions we'd had. Come to find out, he'd only claimed to enjoy Shakespeare to get on the teacher's favorite list. But a few weeks later Donald felt so bad about his deception that he confessed it to the teacher."

Caleb chuckled.

"Hanging out with him, Donald worked his magic and got on my favorite list too. Things moved fast once he noticed me, and the more I got to know him, the more I respected him. I should have guessed that someone that honest and idealistic would make a dumb decision because he felt it was honorable . . ." Millie paused and turned to Caleb. "Do you know what *idealistic* is?"

"*Ja*, I did go to school."

"Yes, but only to eighth grade, and in my mind *idealistic* is a high school word." Millie chuckled.

"And the dumb decision?"

"Everyone around us was talking about the military. It was on the radio and on everyone's mind at school."

"Was that World War II?"

Millie's mouth fell open. She fixed her eyes on Caleb, and then she picked up her hat from the bench and whacked him with it. "How old do you think I am, son? I'm talking about Vietnam."

The horses whinnied, as if giving their approval.

"Sorry, Millie. You're right. That eighth-grade education is lacking sometimes."

Was Millie going to have a point to this story? Did she ever have a point?

"I know what you're thinking. You're thinking that I don't have a point—that I'm just flapping my gums. But there is a point." She looked at him and pursed her lips. "I have not always agreed with Donald's decisions. When he joined the military, I thought he was a goner for sure. I was a total mess until he got home.

"But it wasn't like things were perfect after that. There were things that annoyed me about him. There were things I nagged him about until the day he died. For instance, he'd set the alarm for six o'clock in the morning, but he kept hitting the snooze alarm until seven. No matter how many times I'd tell him, 'Donald, you don't get up until seven o'clock! Don't set the alarm until then,' he kept setting it for the same time." Millie crossed her arms. "He had good intentions, but no morning resolve. He never listened." Millie lowered her head, and her voice softened. "No, he never listened."

"Sounds like something I'd do . . . So, what happened to him, Millie?"

"He died in a logging accident. Old fool—he shouldn't have been out there with all those young bucks. One morning he left with his coffee thermos and a smile, and a few hours later he was gone. Of course, it didn't seem real until the next morning." Her words caught in her throat. "At six o'clock . . . well, that alarm went blaring off, and at that moment I would have done anything, given anything, to have that fool lying by me, hitting the snooze and then falling back asleep. Even all these years later I still haven't been able to change that alarm. It wakes me up—losing Donald woke me up—and when I hear its blaring, I start praying. I pray that God will give me a truly thankful heart. I pray that I won't take anyone—or any of God's good gifts—for granted."

"I hear what you're saying, Millie, but Rebecca lied to me. She put on Amish clothes when her intention this whole time has been to go to nursing school."

"Yes, yes, she did lie." Millie nodded. "And if I were you, I'd take that as a compliment."

"Are you kidding?"

"Not at all. That girl's mind was set. Her eyes were fixed on leaving her Amish ways behind and then going to nursing school. But something caused her to pause." Millie cleared her throat. "Or should I say *someone*."

Caleb removed his hat and set it on the wagon bench, and then he scratched his head.

"Sometimes we believe what we think is right is what *is* right," Millie said. "We believe that if we're bothered by something, it's justified, but when we really take time and think about what we deserve—well, the minor interruptions don't matter. You don't deserve love, Caleb. I didn't either. No one does. We're all failures when it comes to living selflessly, but that doesn't mean that sometimes love doesn't come and surprise us. It's a gift from God, I think.

"You've already been chosen," Millie continued. "First you were chosen by God. And then you were chosen by a young woman whose heart is bigger than the weight of her. You were chosen to be given a chance. And no, Rebecca didn't do everything right, but none of us do."

Millie reached over and flicked the side of Caleb's head. It stung and he winced. "Hey, what was that for?"

"Consider that your wake-up call, son. And next time I won't be so gentle."

Millie sat quietly after that, which was making even more of a statement. Millie wanted him to think. Really think. And she wasn't going to let him off easy.

It took the alarm story for Caleb to realize that he was being *dumm*. He'd needed that wake-up call, and he was thankful Millie was here to give it to him. He shuddered to think of how he'd almost thrown in the towel on someone he'd grown to care about, for the mere fact that his pride was hurt. Rebecca had lied, but he hadn't always been truthful, had he? She still didn't know about everything. What would Rebecca do if she knew he'd abandoned his responsibilities in Ohio? She might have thought twice about coming on this trip, about befriending him.

The ride was quiet, and when they parked the wagon for lunch, Caleb turned to Millie. "I've been a fool, Millie."

She reached over and patted his hand. "Yes, and now that

we both agree, I think there's someone you need to talk to."
Millie pointed, and Caleb followed her gaze. Amos was offering Rebecca a hand as she climbed down from the wagon.

Caleb jumped down and jogged her direction, but before
he got to her, he paused, noticing tears in her eyes. What had
Rebecca and Annie been talking about? Seeing that, Caleb
backed away. She was probably crying about him—how he'd
treated her. He didn't blame her. Instead of walking up to her,
Caleb turned to Ike.

"Do you need help with anything?" he called.

Rebecca sat in her tent with tears sliding down her cheeks. She
rubbed her eyes, wondering how yesterday's perfect day with
Caleb had turned into one of the worst of her life. The only
thing she'd been thankful for was that she'd been able to ride
in the wagon with Annie and talk with her. Maybe it was the
fact that Annie knew Rebecca wasn't going to stay around the
West Kootenai area long that she told Rebecca the truth about
Robert's death and how he'd been killed in a motorcycle accident. Annie had cried as she'd told her, and Rebecca couldn't
help but cry too. It seemed a shame that someone died who'd
had so much potential . . . just like Claudia.

The pain in her heart was heavy, and as she sat there,
Rebecca remembered what Millie had said. Rebecca zipped
open her suitcase. She didn't have a box that she could tuck
prayers into, but she did have the secret compartment in her
suitcase that still had room.

She pulled out one of her notebooks she'd had for school
and tore out a few blank pages. Then she tore those into little
pieces and began writing.

Lord, I don't know what I'm supposed to do with these feelings for Caleb. Show me.

Dear God, Annie is afraid to love again. Soften her heart, and give her wisdom over what to do with Ike's being Amish.

God, please help Marianna's boppli *to stick.* Rebecca had stolen that prayer request from Millie, but she couldn't think of a better way to put it.

Lord, when I get to civilization, give me the courage to call home. I know I shouldn't have left like that. Help me to be brave and to tell the truth.

As she wrote each one, she tucked it into the secret spot. With each one she tucked, she made it a point to picture herself lifting her hands to God, offering up her worries.

Outside the tent she heard voices, and she knew that she couldn't hide away for long. If anything, that was one thing she'd discovered on this journey: one couldn't hide away in a small group of people. It was easy to be missed. Not that she minded. If anything, it had caused Rebecca to look at herself in ways she never had before.

CHAPTER

20

They'd had a quiet dinner, each one lost in his or her own thoughts, it seemed. Ike and Amos built a fire, and just as Rebecca was going to find a log to roll in front of it for a seat, Caleb asked if she wanted to go for a walk. She joined him, wondering if she was going to get another talking-to. Instead Caleb's demeanor was hesitant, and his voice was gentle as he spoke.

"I've been talking to Millie."

Rebecca wrapped her arms around herself. "Well, I'd like to think so. I can't imagine you'd be riding along with her for any length of time without having a good conversation."

"I'm only going to tell you this once, Rebecca. I've been a fool. *Ja*, I'm upset because you lied to me, but Millie told me I should be impressed that you should think so much of me that you'd put up such a hoax."

"Oh, it's a hoax now?"

"Well, okay, maybe that's a strong word, but you have to tell me . . . Why did you do it? Why did you decide to wear your Amish clothes again? Why did you want to *kumme* along?"

"*Vell*, it was hard leaving everything at once—my family

and friends, my clothes and my culture. I didn't know how to be *Englisch*. I thought it would bring freedom not having my Amish clothes with me, but the opposite is true. Freedom is being comfortable in the clothes you're in."

"And I had nothing to do with it?"

She glanced up at him and wrinkled her nose. "*Vell*, maybe just a little."

"So do you want to tell me more . . . about nursing school?" He paused, and she turned to him. "I want to listen," he said.

Rebecca blushed but her gaze held steady. "It seems silly to me whenever I talk about it. I have no special talents, and my community and beliefs tell me that this is not an occupation I need to pursue, but the idea that I could help someone—even one person—fuels me. And I know that when I help one person, I'm helping their whole family too. All of us were affected by Claudia's death. I just think if I don't do this, if I don't pursue it, I'll always regret it. If I ever have the chance to help another person and I can't . . . Well, that seems even more tragic than Claudia's death."

They walked together in the sun. The forest was thinner here, and it looked as if it had been logged in recent years. Her dat had once told her that cutting out the scraggly trees gave the good ones more room, more light. And it had taken getting away from Indiana—all the people, concerns, and distractions—to really start considering not just what she wanted to do with her life, but who she wanted in it.

"I've always wanted something like that—a passion, a mission." He spoke solemnly. "I'm jealous for it. I've never had something that's completely grabbed ahold of my heart, and seeing that in you has made me care more, not less. You were afraid of telling me the truth, but the truth is who you are. And maybe you had reason to be afraid. I didn't handle things well, and I'm sorry. But Millie talked some sense into me. She even gave me a good thump on the side of my head. I've been a fool for putting thoughts of myself above thoughts of you, Rebecca. I want to know all of you. I want to know more."

They returned to their walking, and Rebecca told herself to enjoy this moment. To soak in the beauty. To soak in Caleb being next to her. To get over being mad, hurt.

The woods were littered with dead leaves, decaying pine-cones. They stepped over logs and walked around bushes. The sky was a brighter blue than it had been, and every now and then Rebecca would see a spot of color—the pink of a wild rose, the red of Indian paintbrush, white daisies tiny and delicate. And then the trees bunched up again, branches stretched down, and they stepped into the arms of shade. She walked over ground splotchy with patches of shade and light. What would happen next? What would become of them? When their wagon train ended, they'd be heading two separate ways.

Her attention shifted to Caleb, and she watched him stride beside her as if he didn't have a care in the world. Concern tightened her throat—concern that she'd be a burden. That if anything grew between them it would narrow his future. After all, an Amishman could not love her without consequences.

"I'm sorry. I don't know what to say to you. It hurts my brain just thinking about where we can go from here," she finally said.

"Then stop thinking about it. Can you just enjoy the moment, Rebecca, without having to try to figure everything out?"

She sat on the closest fallen tree and then lowered her gaze. "*Ja*, I suppose so."

"What's the matter?"

"Nothing. I'm just happy that you asked me to walk with you. I'm thankful that you listened to Millie."

"You're not acting like you're happy."

"I am, very much."

"May I sit beside you?"

"*Ja*, of course."

He sat close. Close enough that their legs nearly touched.

"I talked to Annie this morning. She still doesn't think it's right that she ask Ike to leave the Amish." Rebecca didn't tell him what else they talked about—about Robert's death.

He took her hand. "Let's not talk about Annie, or Ike. Is that fine? At least for a few minutes."

His hand squeezed hers tighter and then pulled it toward him. He leaned forward and kissed the top of it. She'd kissed three boys on the lips before, all *Englisch* and all trouble, but none of those kisses caused her heart to pound like it did now.

She reached up with her free hand and touched his cheek, noticing how smooth it was from his morning shave and picturing a beard—a beard that would grow after their wedding, telling the world he belonged to her. Rebecca shook her head slightly. No, that was the Amish way. If she were—if they were—*Englisch*, there'd be no reason for him to grow a beard.

Even though it made sense, something pinched her heart at the thought of it.

"Caleb," she said softly.

He lifted his head and their eyes met.

"I don't want you to think I pushed you into this. That I spilled my heart so that you'd be forced to respond. That you'd have to make wild statements—"

He scooted closer. "And you think you're the one pushing me into this?"

His breath caressed her cheek, spreading warmth from her chest through her limbs.

"You don't think, Rebecca, that I've thought about this? That as we rode along over the last few days I didn't consider what it would be like to kiss you—to tell you that I think you're beautiful and I've never known anyone like you?"

Heat rose to her cheeks. "That's how the *Englisch* talk."

"*Vell*, I guarantee that's how many Amishmen feel. They just don't have the nerve to tell the women they're falling for. Instead they just stare at them over the fire at a Youth Singing, or they offer to drive them home and ask for a date. I've never been like that. I've never been one to hold back." Caleb cleared his throat. "Believe me, I have a lot more to say too—"

The sound of footsteps and voices coming through the woods interrupted his words, and without hesitation he pulled back. She dropped her fingers from his cheek, and he released her hand. Passion heated his gaze, and she smiled. His words were braver than his actions.

Voices drifted to them, and footsteps crunched pinecones. Caleb scooted over, putting a few more inches between them, yet that did little to settle the stirring of her heart.

Caleb cleared his throat. "We better head back."

Rebecca nodded and rose. She adjusted her *kapp*, wondering if she should even wear it now. It wasn't as if she was fooling anyone. Maybe if she did dress in *Englisch* clothes, Caleb would understand—really understand—what he was getting himself into. As long as she wore Amish clothes and acted like she always had, he wouldn't see her as who she was now—or at least who she was in the process of becoming.

On their walk back they met Annie and Millie.

"We thought about heading up to the lake that's just over those hills, but Ike thinks we should hang around another day and attempt that tomorrow," Millie said. "It wouldn't be fun to get stuck hiking around these mountains in the dark."

"So instead, we were hoping to find some wild mushrooms. They would add flavor to the rice for tomorrow's dinner," Annie added. "But we're not having any luck."

"I'm not sure if I'd eat a wild mushroom." Caleb wrinkled his nose. "Mushrooms haven't been a favorite."

"Oh, so you're going to be picky about my cooking now, are you?" Annie chuckled. "Let's see if you'll have a log to sit on tonight . . . and a tin plate to eat from."

"Maybe it's the fact that I'm the only boy in a family of girls. I was a bit spoiled, although my mem would never admit it. My *opa* and *oma* lived with us, and whenever there was something I didn't like, *Opa* would say, 'Gertie, he's big and strong without eating that.' I got away with too much, I think."

Rebecca chuckled, but she could see a cloud falling over Caleb's face as he talked about his *opa*. She knew his loss was great. *And look at me, acting as if I'm the only one who's ever lost someone I've loved.* She glanced from face to face in their small circle, realizing they'd all faced loss.

Caleb pointed his thumbs to his chest. "*Ja*, no mushrooms for this guy. Just know what you're getting into now, Rebecca. I do torment all those I care about."

Hearing him say her name pulled her attention back to the conversation, realizing that he'd just admitted his care caused heat to rise to her cheeks.

But do you have any idea what you're getting yourself into now, Caleb?

Rebecca turned and headed back toward their campsite with a little hop in her step. She did believe he cared, she could see it in his eyes, but before they got on the wagon trail again, Caleb needed to understand what he was really signing himself up for.

Caleb retired to the tent that night to find Amos waiting. Amos had a cross look on his face, and Caleb tried to ignore it. He couldn't get his mind off of Rebecca's hand on his cheek. It caused his stomach to warm even now.

"I think you've got some explaining to do." Amos' voice was terse.

"Do I owe you an apology for something?" Caleb glanced over at his friend. Then he snapped his fingers. "I'm sorry I didn't have more insight to invite a younger, prettier companion for you on this trip—"

"I'm not talking about me."

"What do you mean?"

"You have some explaining to do with Rebecca. You were upset, really upset with her today, but have you told her yet about your *opa*? About what's happening at home?"

"Listen." Caleb leaned in close, pushing his finger into Amos' chest. "That's nonc of your business."

"Really? Well, I care for her too . . . as a friend. And I think if she's going to be honest about who she is and what you should expect, then you should do the same."

"It's not like I abandoned my family." Caleb lowered his voice. "They told me I needed a break. That I needed to enjoy Montana while I'm still young and have the chance. Besides, I'm sending money home . . ."

"Yes, well, then, if it's no big deal, why haven't you told her already?" Amos stuck his legs into his sleeping bag and slipped down. "It seems to me that neither of you want to return to what you left—for completely different reasons." Amos fixed his eyes on Caleb's. "And only her reason is noble."

CHAPTER
21

Caleb swung the ax, and Rebecca watched, fascinated by his slender frame, wide shoulders, and flexing chest. The pile of wood was already up to his knees, but he didn't seem close to pausing. Though his body worked hard, she could tell that his mind was fixed on something else. He seemed lost in thought. Was he thinking about her—thinking of what she'd confessed? Thinking of her leaving . . . heading to Portland and maybe leaving the Amish for good?

Caleb picked up a log and balanced it on the stump. Standing back, he lifted the ax and swung down hard. It hit dead center. He jerked the ax back and followed the same motion. This time the log split in two.

"I think you have enough wood for every campsite in the Kootenais," she chuckled.

Caleb glanced over at her, and his eyes grew wide. "Mornin', yourself."

Caleb paused with the ax in his hand and looked to Rebecca. His breath caught in his throat. Instead of the Amish dress and *kapp* she'd been wearing, today her dark hair hung loose over her shoulders. She wore hiking boots and jeans. She'd found his thick plaid jacket that he'd been wearing last night and had put it on.

"Yer . . . yer not in Amish dress."

Rebecca shrugged. "I realized that it wasn't any use pretending. Everyone knows the truth."

He imagined her getting on the train at the Whitefish train station. He imagined her getting to Portland and taking a taxi to her college. He imagined her showing up for classes for the first time since being in an Amish school when she was fourteen, and he'd never been so proud of another person. She was so brave.

Caleb realized he'd been staring and rubbed a hand along his jaw. He leaned on his ax and reached down for his hat, placing it firmly on his head.

"If you want to get a fire started with some of that wood, I can start on breakfast. You don't mind, do you?" she asked.

"No, ma'am." He winked at her. He took up an armful of wood and headed to the campfire area. Rebecca waited patiently, basking in the golden morning light. Overhead a dozen birds flitted from tree to tree. He watched as Rebecca gazed up, noticing their song too.

She looked at him and smiled. "What are you staring at?"

He shook his head, feeling his face heat. "Nothing."

"Do I look strange in these men's clothes?" She glanced down. "I hope you don't mind me borrowing your jacket. It's just a bit cold out here."

"You don't look anything like a man, that's for certain, Rebecca."

Instead of answering him, Rebecca turned. "Do you know where the others are?"

"They headed up to the lake about an hour ago to catch

fish for lunch. Millie was in a hurry to get up there, so I told Ike I'd take care of everything around here. Annie wanted to invite you, but I told her that you'd rather have sleep."

"Then you know me well."

Caleb took care as he laid the logs and kindling, lit a match, and watched the sticks flare. When the fire took off, he stood and wiped his hands on his thighs.

He could see her breath on the air, and the crispness made him feel alive. He couldn't imagine returning to Ohio. Yes, the rolling hills were beautiful, but nothing like this. More than that, he couldn't imagine returning to the community he'd grown up in and trying to find a bride among all the women there. Not after he'd been with Rebecca. There was no one like her there. He'd never met anyone like her.

They heated up some of the leftovers Annie had saved for them, and then Caleb told her he was going to head out to the pasture to check on the horses before going up to the lake.

"Did you hear the wolves last night?" he asked.

"How could I have missed them? But they sounded far away."

"Closer than you might think," Caleb commented, striding down the road to where the horses were.

"I'll join you," she called.

"Okay, but I need to talk to you about something later today when we head out." He tried to make his voice sound serious, but it was hard when he was smiling. "The truth is, maybe you should ride with Annie and Ike today; they have that second seat. I can move some of their gear into my wagon."

"What—what's wrong?" She hurried next to him. It took two of her steps to keep up with his one. "It's the clothes, isn't it? It's hitting you, right?"

"Just the opposite, Rebecca." He paused and turned to her. "I've never been so proud of anyone for what you're doing. And . . ." He took a deep breath. Did he dare say the rest? He thought against it, but the words wouldn't be held back. "And I've never seen you look so beautiful."

"Then why are you running from me?"

"Maybe it's not you I'm running from."

Rebecca didn't ask what he was talking about. Instead they approached the nearest pasture and looked around. His eyes scanned the high mountain pasture, and his stomach knotted up. Caleb couldn't believe what he was seeing. Nothing. The horses were gone. He removed his hat and tossed it onto the ground. "It must have been those wolves . . ."

"They got the horses?" Fear clung to Rebecca's words.

Caleb's stomach lurched, and he thought he was going to be sick.

"They didn't get them, but they scared them off." He picked up his hat and dusted it off. "Who knows where they are now? And that means we're not going anywhere until we find them."

Caleb led her on a wide sweep around the pasture. The ground was soft and the prints of the horses' hooves made no sense to her.

"How in the world are you going to find out which direction they went?" she asked.

"Well, we know they didn't head up the road—we would have heard them. And from what I can see, they didn't head down the road. But look here . . ." He walked to a wide spot in the trees, pointing to an opening. "See how there are a lot more prints here? They must have been prancing in this area for a while. Then they headed in there."

Caleb pointed, and she looked deeper into the wooded area. Sure enough, there were horses' footprints deeper into the forest.

"You found which way they went!" Excitement bubbled up from inside. "I just hope they didn't go too far," she said. "It seems like they could run forever in these mountains."

"Oh, I'm sure they got shook up by those howls we heard, but they're not runners. They're usually good at sticking by home, and once the initial jolt got them going, they probably realized they'd strayed too far. Hopefully they're staying put."

They walked along the path, away from the lake. Rebecca was only partly sad that she wouldn't be seeing it. The truth was, she'd rather spend her day with Caleb.

"Do you know that tomorrow we'll be in Libby?" he said. "I'm looking forward to gas station doughnuts and one of those Slushee drinks. But don't tell Annie."

"I was wondering about that. I figured we were getting close. And when I get there, there's something I need to do."

"Yeah, what's that?" he asked, brushing a tree branch out of the way for her to walk under.

"I need to call home. I need to tell my parents where I am and how I'm headed to Portland in just a couple weeks."

"A couple weeks?" He stopped short. "That soon?"

"My classes in Portland start in three weeks. I need at least a week there to get used to the city and settle in."

"So, are you excited?"

"Scared. It's a big city—a couple million people." She thought about what Millie had said earlier. "It's a beautiful city, or so a customer at the bakery told me."

"Why did you choose Portland of all places to move to?" He

eyed the trampled brush that the horses had pushed through. His voice quivered, and he wore a pained expression.

She swallowed hard. "Well, first I wanted to see the Pacific Ocean. So many people travel to Pinecraft and see the Gulf of Mexico there—I just wanted to be different." She chuckled. "I suppose I've always wanted to be different.

"But there was another reason too," she confessed. "It's because of the name . . . and the memories."

"Portland?" Caleb scratched his head. "It's not all that pretty of a name."

"*Vell*, I remember one year my grandparents took Claudia and me to the Parke County Covered Bridge Festival. There are a few dozen covered bridges there, and our favorite was the Portland Mills Bridge. It was the oldest, yet they'd just renovated it. I liked that. It seemed right that they fixed up the old structure instead of tearing it down. I remember it had been raining, yet inside Claudia and I were safe and dry. That's when she told me that covered bridges were kissing bridges. She was four years older, so she already had her eyes set on who she wanted to be kissing. I just liked the idea of it, and I promised myself right then that I was going to find a beau who would sneak a kiss in a bridge just like that. You think I'm silly . . . don't you?"

"I think you're a girl."

"What does that mean?"

"It means that I will never understand girls. I determined that when I was six years old, and every day has confirmed it. But I do know that it's a beautiful thought—a beautiful memory. *Danki* for sharing it."

They hiked for ten minutes, and then they heard the whinnying. They entered a clearing, and Caleb spoke a soft greeting. Nearing the animals, he patted Millie's black gelding on the rump. Caleb's horse approached, as if thankful to be found, and Caleb turned and patted him on his wide forehead.

"We should have brought leads," Rebecca commented.

"Are you kidding? I'm pretty sure they'll follow us out." He gave Millie's horse a solid slap on the rump and then started walking back the way they'd come. The horses followed, and Rebecca marveled at his assuredness that the animals wouldn't give them any trouble.

They walked through the woods, and the horses did a good job making a line, as if they were on a trail ride.

"I'm thankful for this time again," she said. "Thankful that we have time to be together and that we're on speaking terms."

Caleb looked at her and raised his eyebrows, and then he reached down and entwined his fingers through hers, squeezing. "'Speaking terms.' Is that what you call it?"

"Well, sure. I'm just sorry . . ." She kicked at a pinecone. "I'm sorry that I wasn't more truthful from the beginning. As I think about how I just left my parents like that, and how I deceived you, I have many regrets. I just didn't think there was another way, especially with my parents. I felt helpless, in a way. I knew if they found out, they'd stop me from going."

"Do you think you're the only one with regrets, Rebecca? Do you think you're the only one who's felt helpless before?"

He looked at her and took a deep breath, as if he was preparing to release words that he'd stored up inside for a while. "It was last year my *opa* had a stroke, and he couldn't talk, and hardly could move. My mem would set him in a stupid rocking chair on the front porch. She told me he enjoyed the sunshine, and I wanted to tell her that she was crazy. Before his stroke, he never sat still. Everything in his barn was in order. His fields were tended. The animals looked as if they'd just been prepped for showing in the county fair.

"Without his set of hands, I tried to keep up, but I couldn't. My dat worked at the factory morning until night, and he was a deacon besides, which is always a lot of work with no extra pay. As the only grandson, everyone knew the farm would someday be mine, and that it was my job. Soon the barn needed to be painted, and we had to get rid of the sheep because they just became too much work. And *Opa* saw it all. He saw all that he'd worked so hard for fall short of his standards. He'd watched me work, and I'd never been so embarrassed."

"When did he die?"

Caleb released her hand and crossed his arms over his chest. His shoulders slumped, and she'd never seen him looking so dejected. "*Ach*—he's not dead yet. In fact, from Mem's last letter he's doing a little better."

"Then why are you here? Why aren't you back there with him? I know how much he means to you."

"I told my dat I had to get out of there. Don't you understand, Rebecca? I don't want to be a disappointment to him. I wasn't able to do it—run the farm like he did. I'll never be able to do it. And . . . if I heard those words . . . If he ever had to tell me that I wasn't doing a very good job . . . Well, I don't think I could take it."

"You need to go back, Caleb. You need to see him, spend time with him. If he loves you, then I'm sure he'd rather see your face than worry about if you have the tack hanging on the right hooks in the barn." Her heart pounded. Rebecca would do anything for simply one more day with Claudia. Just to sit beside her, laugh, and tell her all about Claude's antics, especially how he always hid his peas in his napkin just like his mother used to do.

"*Opa* was the one who always told me that he wished he'd

seen more of the world," Caleb continued. "He told me a thousand times that he wished he'd taken more risks. He probably never traveled more than twenty-five miles from his farm his whole life. He was a *gut* Amishman. I tell myself that I'm doing this for him—living the life that he couldn't."

"I think that's just an excuse. I think what you said about not wanting to disappoint him is an excuse too. I can see it in your eyes."

"See what?"

"Fear. You are afraid of your *opa* dying and not being there. But maybe you're even more afraid of him living as a shell of the person that he used to be. It's not easy to see that. Because when we do, we have to face the fact that our lives are only a vapor too. And then we have to wonder about the hereafter . . . and if we're doing enough to please God."

She paused and picked up a pinecone, turning it over in her hands. "But it's not our doing that matters, is it? It's accepting what Jesus has already done. It's seeing Him—and Him alone—as the way to eternity with God."

"You seem to know a lot these days. When did you get all the answers?"

"I don't have all the answers, but I've been paying attention and listening. This trip has changed me, Caleb. The people have changed me more—more than I thought they ever would."

They got the horses back to the right pasture. What would tomorrow bring? They sat in the pasture awhile, taking in the gentle breeze and the happy grazing of the horses. Rebecca couldn't help but wonder about what her mem would say, what her dat would say, about where she was and what she'd been doing. They would like Caleb—that she knew—but the rest of it? They'd feel their daughter was following the ways of the world for sure, and they'd find themselves among the ranks of those who'd lost their children to the world's grasp. To lose a child by death was sad, but to lose a child to the enemy's ways—that was a tragedy.

CHAPTER
22

They had a dinner of baked potatoes and hot dogs on sticks, roasted over the fire. They looked at photos on Annie's digital camera that she took that day of the beautiful lake high in the mountains and then tried to pick out the constellations in the vast night sky. Rebecca wished there was a button she could use to slow down time. She didn't want this night to end. She didn't want to face the fact that in the morning she'd be calling her parents, hearing their disappointment. She simply wanted to live in this moment of wearing *Englisch* clothes and being just as accepted as when she wore Amish dress. She wanted to soak in Caleb's eyes upon her. She wanted to laugh at Millie's stories and then listen to them again. She wanted to enjoy Caleb and Amos as they teased each other and smirk at the loving gazes that Annie and Ike cast each other over the fire pit—gazes they tried unsuccessfully to hide.

One by one the others went to sleep until it was just Rebecca and Caleb sitting before the fire.

"It's been a good journey, and then we have the trip home," Caleb said. "More time to talk—at least a few more days until you head to Portland."

"What then?" Rebecca picked up small stones and lined them up in a straight line on her jeans. She had to do something to keep her mind occupied rather than looking into Caleb's handsome face. Every time she did, joy fought against sadness. They cared for each other, that was true, but they wouldn't be able to be together . . . not with her in Portland and him here in Montana.

"What are you thinking about?" he asked, pulling her from her thoughts.

"I was trying to think of when I'll be able to see you again. Maybe during the Christmas holiday I can ride the train back here. If I can find some type of part-time job, that is. Right now I barely have enough money to live on." She didn't tell him about where that money had come from. She hadn't told anyone about it.

"What about letters . . . until we see each other? I'm not much for writing, but I can learn."

"*Ja*, but can they carry us through the span of years?"

Caleb's eyes widened. "Years? I don't want to wait that long."

"That's how long nursing school takes."

"No." He shook his head. "I don't like that at all. I don't know how I'll be able to deal with you so far away. But I've never felt so alive. I've never shared so much of my heart."

"It's the fresh mountain air." Her voice was no more than a whisper. Then she chuckled. "And you'll still have that after I'm gone." She brushed the rocks from her legs with one swoop, and then she looked at him. "Just breathe deeply."

"If you're going to use that excuse, then I can blame that very same air on making me do this."

The touch of Caleb's hand on her cheek made her stomach feel as fluid as Mem's plum jam before it set up. He scooted closer, but a knot in the log they were sitting on still kept him too far to lean forward for a kiss. She told herself not to lean forward. She told herself she'd regret it and she didn't want to hurt him. But there was love, real love, that radiated from Caleb's gaze. And for the first time in years—more years than she could count—she wanted to let herself feel it.

Rebecca leaned forward and allowed him to offer her a quick peck. Their lips barely touched before she pulled back. She wanted him to hold her. She wanted to cuddle in his embrace, but for the first time in a long time, Rebecca tried to think of someone else besides herself. Getting too close physically would just make it harder when they parted. It would also make it harder to hold back in the future. For now one soft kiss was enough. Caleb could read the rest of her care just by looking into her eyes.

Rebecca could tell that the clerk from Mac's Market wasn't expecting three wagons to pull up during the a.m. shift. That morning had been the worst part of the journey so far. They'd moved from old logging roads onto the paved two-lane road, and while people in Indiana were used to seeing buggies and wagons on the road, they seemed to distract the tourists in this part of Montana. Even worse were those cars that slowed way down to take a picture. Seeing them, Rebecca was thankful she wasn't in Amish dress.

The clerk watched them through the window. Her eyes widened as the three wagons pulled up and parked.

Amos jumped down from the wagon and waved. "What would she do if we went in and told her we need her to fill up our rigs?" The others chuckled.

But while the others also felt satisfied that they'd made it through half of their journey, a sinking feeling rested in Rebecca's gut. Being at the gas station told her one thing: that they'd have cell service. And that meant it was time to call home.

She used the restroom, thankful to have access to a toilet again, and then approached Annie, who was filling up a fountain drink.

"Annie, can I borrow your, uh, cell phone?"

Annie didn't ask any questions and Rebecca was thankful.

Rebecca went outside and rounded the side of the building, then dialed the number to her parents' phone that they kept outside in a phone shack near the road. The phone was supposed to be just for emergencies—they'd put it in after Claudia's death—but Mem often went out and checked the messages as soon as she heard it ring. The phone was off limits to the younger kids, especially Claude—lest they get too accustomed to having it and decide to put one in their own homes someday.

The phone rang three times, and then the answering machine picked up.

"Mem, this is Rebecca. I am sorry I left and didn't tell you my plans. The letter explained some, Mem, but there is so much more to tell you. I'm . . . I am sure you are worried. There is a cell phone you can call, if you'd like to reach me." She left Annie's number. When she looked up, Caleb stood at the corner of the building, watching.

"Are you all right?" he asked.

"If anyone's home they'll call back right away. My brothers should be doing chores about this time. They can always hear the phone from the barn. They race to get Mem to tell her about the message. They can even make calls for emergencies."

Sure enough, less than four minutes later Annie's phone rang.

Rebecca's fingers trembled slightly as she answered. "*Ja?*"

"Rebecca?" Even though her brother Isaiah was twelve years old, his voice over the phone sounded much younger. "Did you run away? Dat said you did."

She cleared her throat, wondering what else her dat had said. "I left . . . for a while. Is Mem there?"

"*Ne.*"

"Dat?"

"*Ne.* They are both gone. They went on the train . . . to look for you."

Rebecca's jaw dropped open. In a month of Sundays she never expected those words from his mouth.

"But where did they go?"

"Montana."

"And how did they find out where I am?"

"Someone from our district has a cousin. Or maybe a *bruder* there in Montana . . ." Isaiah's voice faded. "Do ya want to talk to *Aenti* Diana? She's here."

"*Ja.*" She blew out a low breath. While Mem and Dat were quiet in nature, her *aenti* was anything but.

"So Adam's Betty says yer in Montana." Her aunt's voice rattled on as if she was chatting about the weather.

"*Ja.* That's right. I was calling to apologize. I'd written a letter. I don't know if they got it. *Aenti* . . . I'm sorry. I didn't mean for them to worry." Rebecca felt ten again. The tenseness radiating through her reminded her of when she'd dropped her aunt's seeds and gotten them mixed up. Even though she'd hidden the truth, it had been found out when the radishes started popping up with the green beans, and vice versa.

"It's *Oma*'s fault." Her aunt tsk-tsked.

"What?" Rebecca's jaw dropped. "What did you say?"

She could hear her *aenti*'s sigh even over the phone line. "If she hadn't let you have those dreams of becoming a nurse . . . if she hadn't given you that money, why, this never would have happened."

"But, *Aenti*, how did you know?"

Caleb's eyes, filled with concern, watched her as she spoke. He placed a hand on her shoulder, most likely for support, but it was making her nervous to have him there as she tried to figure out how her *aenti* had known about the money, about the schooling.

"She was my mem, and she lived with me. And she was a talker. Do you think she could have kept that a secret?"

Rebecca gasped. "But why didn't you say anything?"

"Who am I to talk? I saw what Claudia's death did to you. After that, I never expected you to stay. I hoped, but I didn't expect it. I just never thought you'd go so far."

"And Mem and Dat?"

"They went to Montana just like Isaiah said. They went to stay with your friend Marianna. They got her number from Naomi and made the call."

Rebecca leaned her back against the cold concrete of the gas station. "*Danki*, then. I'm sure I'll see them soon. It was *gut* to hear your voice, *Aenti*, but I do have to go."

"Rebecca . . ." Her *aenti's* voice drew her back.

"What?"

"Rebecca, remember one thing: your parents have already lost a daughter. Don't leave them without hope that someday they'll get you back too."

"I'm not gone forever, *Aenti*. I simply have to get the schooling I need to *kumme* back, to help."

"That's *gut*. I'll make sure you keep your word concerning that. *Ja*, Rebecca, that's very *gut*."

CHAPTER

23

It didn't take them long to find Ben and Marianna. When the wagons pulled into the Cabinet Mountain Campground, Ben's truck was already waiting.

Rebecca was the first off the wagon, and she hurried over to the truck. She expected to see her parents sitting in the backseat of his extended cab, but she was glad they weren't there.

Their wagons had been due in yesterday, but they'd taken an extra day for the others to hike to the lake. How long had Ben and Marianna been waiting for them to arrive? Had they been worried? Had her parents been worried? She had no doubt they were.

Ben looked to be asleep in the driver's seat. He was leaning against the window with a sweatshirt tucked under his chin. Marianna was in the front seat reading a book. Well, at least the book was open in her lap, but her mind seemed to be someplace else. She looked to be the same sweet Marianna Rebecca had always known, except unlike their growing-up years she wore a head scarf instead of a *kapp*. Rebecca approached and tapped on the window. Marianna jumped, and then relief flooded her face. She put up her book and then swung open the door.

"There you are . . . You had us worried. I thought you were supposed to get to Libby yesterday."

"Well, we were, but there were a few issues."

"Nothing serious I hope."

"No, not at all."

"And I think you forgot something." Marianna held up Rebecca's cell phone.

Rebecca gladly accepted it. "I'm so glad you brought that." She resisted the urge to check to see if she had any messages.

Ben stirred awake and then hurried into motion, jumping out of the truck to help the others with the horses.

"No serious issues, I hope."

"A broken wheel, a wound I needed to bandage, the side trip to the lake, and lost horses . . . among a few other things."

She eyed Marianna, taking her hand. Rebecca wanted to ask about her parents, but she had to find out something else first. "Marianna . . . how are you feeling? How's the *boppli*?"

Marianna's hand covered her stomach, and her face lit up. "Very well. We went to the doctor in Kalispell. We heard the heartbeat and got the ultrasound. I wanted to bring the photo to show you, but Ben was afraid we'd lose it. He already has it framed, and he's calling our little one Bean . . . because that's what the ultrasound looks like."

Rebecca offered her friend a quick hug. "I'm so glad."

Marianna pulled back and eyed her. "You look different. Happy, I think. Happier than I've seen you in a while. And where are your Amish clothes?"

"Let's just say that I lost layers on this trip. You really have to just be who you are. It's not possible to put on a show for very long when you're with friends like this, in the middle of a wilderness." Rebecca sighed. "But . . . I have to ask: have you seen my parents? I called home to talk to them and—"

"*Ja,* they are here." Marianna bit her lip. "They were so worried. I had to tell them—"

Rebecca placed a hand on Marianna's arm. "They are here?" She glanced around.

"Not here at the campground. But they are here in Libby—at a hotel. They arrived on the train two days ago, and we got here yesterday. They are resting . . . and probably praying."

"I think we should go see them," Rebecca said.

"Okay, let me go talk to Ben." Marianna hurried over to him. They talked for a few minutes, and then she came back. "Ben's going to stay here and help the others set up their things while I drive you over."

Marianna nodded. She moved to the truck and climbed into the driver's seat, but before she started the engine, she turned in Rebecca's direction. "Do you want to get your suitcase?"

"Why? Do you think that Dat is going to kidnap me and take me back to Indiana?"

"No . . . but if you wanted to put on your Amish dress, we could stop at a gas station."

Rebecca blew out a slow breath, considering her words, understanding Marianna's concern. Her parents were already worried about her as it was. Seeing her in *Englisch* clothes would be like another jab to their hearts.

"Actually, I'm not going to worry about that now. I'm still planning to go to Portland, to go to school, no matter what they think." She slammed her door shut and put on her seatbelt. Marianna started the engine.

"I'm not doing this to hurt them," Rebecca said. "I'm doing this to help . . . well, help our community."

"*Ja,* well, I'm not sure they'll see it that way."

They rode through town, and it felt strange to be sitting

inside a vehicle after riding along on a wagon so long. The truck seemed so tall, and it went so fast. And it seemed even odder that a petite person like Marianna could drive it so well.

"Marianna, are you sorry you left?" Rebecca asked as they pulled into a hotel parking lot and parked.

Marianna turned off the engine, but she didn't budge. "I miss it. There are a lot of times it's on my mind. I can't say I'm sorry, but there are days I feel lonely. Days I wish I was back in Shipshe, attending one of those sewing bees I thought were so boring. I suppose what I miss about the community is the feeling of belonging and of truly being known. I see that you have it here in Montana too. The West Kootenai area is a wonderful place. Yet, at the same time, I like not being so fenced in."

"What do you mean?

"For so long it was *us* versus *them*. I felt sorry for the *Englisch*. I felt as if I'd been chosen and they had not. I didn't understand it. Also, I questioned how we could sit and do nothing to share the good news, to get other people to consider being Amish. If I had the truth that could save men's souls, then why wouldn't I share it?"

"So you don't think that by leaving the community—the church—you've put your eternal soul at risk?" Rebecca asked. She thought about what Millie had said. Did Rebecca agree—could Jesus take them across the bridge even if their works didn't match the high standards placed on them by the *Ordnung*?

"I don't think my eternal soul is at risk because I left the Amish. Jest the opposite. I know Jesus more now than I ever did. I love Him more, and I feel His love."

"But the world . . . God's Word says to stay far from it." Rebecca was still trying to put the pieces together in her mind. She placed her hand on the door handle, but she didn't open it. Before she faced her parents, she had to know with certainty.

"It does say that, but it's important to look at who Jesus called 'the world,' Rebecca. That's why reading the Word for yourself is so important. 'The world' is not those who live differently than the Amish church. 'The world' are those who live against God. Who turn their back on Him. Jest think of Annie and some of the other *Englisch* people you've met. Think of Ben. They love God and show it more than most people I've grown up with my entire life."

Rebecca nodded, but it was hard taking the words in. It was as if Marianna was speaking Spanish or Chinese.

"When I first thought of leaving, I'd just accepted the fact that if I was walking away, I was opening myself up to the possibility of going to hell. Yet I hoped that I'd return with the knowledge I needed. And then . . . only then could I one day be safe."

Tears filled Marianna's eyes. "*Vell*, as I heard my dat telling a friend, when we get to heaven we just might be surprised who's there and who's not there."

It took a minute for Rebecca to think about that, and deep down she had a feeling Marianna was right. She'd never met people who loved God as much as Annie and Millie. And they did it without wearing a *kapp*.

"But . . . there is a way you can know, Rebecca. It's not through wearing a *kapp* or being good enough or making sure you stay away from cars and electricity. God's Word says that all of us—everyone from my little sister Ellie to Bishop Shetler—have sinned against God. Yet when we turn to Jesus and confess our sin, He is righteous enough to take away our sin and ensure we have a place in heaven."

Logging trucks rumbled by on the road next to the hotel. Rebecca took in a deep breath, and it smelled more like gasoline than the fresh pine of the last few days. Still, Marianna's words were a fresh breeze, and as Marianna spoke them, it helped to make sense of everything Millie had said. It was good news. Wonderful news.

"It seems too easy to just accept and believe," Rebecca finally said.

"Jesus did the hard part."

"And it doesn't depend on my works?"

"No, Jesus just asks that you love Him with all your heart and follow Him."

"And if I don't? If I live by the world's ways?"

Marianna smiled. "That's not really following Him, is it?"

Rebecca's stomach knotted up. The decision she made at this moment would change everything. Her mem and dat had warned her. Once they'd heard about Marianna leaving the Amish, Rebecca's parents had told her not to communicate with Marianna anymore. *If you talk to her too much, you just might go the way of the world next,* they'd said.

Around their church district, rumors had circulated. Some had said that Marianna was writing letters to her brother, telling Levi to come to Montana with his *fraa*, Naomi. Others were saying that Abe and Ruth Sommer—Marianna's parents—would be leaving the Amish next. But she'd been here, and she'd spent time with them. Instead of their lives causing her to fear, she had hope. More hope in her own good future than she'd ever had before.

Rebecca looked to Marianna. *"'If you hang around them too much, you just might be like them,'"* Rebecca said, mimicking her mem's voice. "That's what my parents warned me every time I wanted to see someone—talk to someone—who'd left the Amish." Rebecca's lips parted slightly. "It's true," she said softly. "I've seen the change in you, Marianna. Being around you has made me want what you have . . . and not jest a handsome husband, although I wouldn't mind one of those too." Rebecca grew serious. "But I do want to believe what you have to say is true . . ."

"We can pray now—do you need me to lead you?" Marianna smiled. "All you have to do is let Jesus know that you choose Him and you believe He's chosen you."

Rebecca shook her head, and then she lowered it. "I think I've got this." Her chest warmed as a few simple sentences emerged from her lips. "Jesus, You were betrayed by the kiss of a friend, and though I've tried to live my life following You, I've also betrayed You in so many ways. Will You forgive me for my sins? I'm ready to take the step, Lord. I know it's only by accepting You as my bridge that I will be able to celebrate with You in eternity after my life here is through."

When she glanced up, there were more tears in Marianna's eyes. "I couldn't have said it better myself." Then she let out a sigh. "Are you ready to go in and see your parents?"

Rebecca wiped at the tears forming in her eyes and nodded. "*Ja*, I think I should . . . but I'm not sure they'll understand."

"They may not, but they love you. Don't you forget that. Them coming here proved it."

Marianna smiled and opened the door of the truck.

Rebecca climbed out of the truck, too, and then she paused. In her mind's eye, she wrote an imaginary note for the conversation to come. She sucked in a large breath and closed her eyes, imagining herself placing it in her newest God box—her heart.

CHAPTER

24

Rebecca took a deep breath, preparing to knock. She paused and turned to Marianna. "Do you remember what Claudia used to do when she was nervous?"

"*Ach, ja,* she'd whistle like a little bird to try to distract herself." Marianna offered a sad smile. "Do you remember how she was afraid of thunderstorms too? Growing up I never wanted to stay over at your house on stormy nights. Between the thunder and the whistling I didn't get a moment of sleep."

Marianna placed a hand on Rebecca's arm. "Just relax and cling to that new hope that's in your heart. Even if your parents don't understand, Rebecca, God is with you. God has a *gut* plan for your life."

Rebecca heard her dat's heavy footsteps approaching the door. He must have heard their voices. She held her breath as the door opened. Then she saw his Amish shirt and suspenders, the long beard—a mix of gray and black—that went to the second button of his shirt. Brown eyes filled now with worry, fear. So familiar, yet foreign here.

"Dat." The word barely escaped her lips.

He took a step toward her, and she thought for a minute he

was going to grab her up in a hug. Instead he paused, looked at her *Englisch* clothes, and his brow furrowed. "Your mem has been worried about you."

"*Ja*, I know." What else could she say? "I am sorry. I didn't handle it well."

"*Kumme*." He motioned for her to enter.

Rebecca walked in and Marianna followed. Seeing the concern on her dat's face at having her friend there, Rebecca turned back to her. "Maybe you should wait in the truck?"

"*Ja*, of course." Marianna leaned forward and offered Rebecca a quick hug. "I'll be praying," she whispered in her ear.

Rebecca stepped farther inside. The room was simple but clean. The best part was a sitting area with a large window overlooking a forested area. Was it just last night that she'd sat on a log by the fire, accepting Caleb's kiss?

Her mem stood up from the chair and turned to Rebecca. Her eyes were red and swollen. More tears came fresh when she saw Rebecca standing there in *Englisch* clothes.

Rebecca wished she could smooth the worry from her mem's mind, blow it away like the puff on a dandelion. She wished she could explain that even though she dressed this way on the outside, her heart had more peace now than it had had in a very long time. But her mother only saw what she wanted to see. Her mother only thought what she'd been raised to know as truth.

Rebecca placed a hand to her neck. Her throat stung, trying to swallow down emotion. The last time she'd seen her mother's eyes so red and swollen had been after Claudia's death. An ache spread through her. At least with Claudia, her parents had hope that Claudia was with God. But her? Her parents thought she was doomed for certain. Rebecca bit her lip, angry at herself for all the worry she had caused.

"Mem, I'm so sorry for hurting you." She rushed over to the chair closest to her mem. "I'm here now. You don't have to worry."

Her mem sank back down into her own chair. "We—we didn't know where you were. Then we heard from Fannie Petershwim that you'd been with your *Englisch* friend, Lora. We finally tracked Lora down, and she told us you were going to Oregon, of all places—to college or some foolhardy place like that. We were relieved when we received word that you were in Montana instead, visiting Marianna. I just don't know why you didn't tell us. Why you left like that. We were so worried, and little Claude . . . He kept crying out, asking for you. We had no idea where you could have gone."

"Mem, didn't you get my letter?" Rebecca asked.

"Letter?"

"I left it in my trunk."

"But why would I go into your trunk?"

Rebecca shrugged. "I don't know. I just thought that you'd try to figure out where I went and you'd look around."

"I don't know why you thought that. I've never been in your trunk."

Rebecca pressed her fingertips to her temple. "Yes, fine. I'm sorry. But I left you a note. I told you that I was leaving . . . for a long time. I told you that I was following what I felt called to do."

"Move to Montana?" her dat butted in. "If you wanted to move, then you should have told us. I—"

"Dat!" Rebecca interrupted. "Lora was right. I left to go to Oregon. Stopping to see Marianna was a decision that I made on the way."

Mem pressed her hands together. "*Ja, vell*, I don't see what appeal Oregon has. We're here now. Marianna said that we can get return tickets home whenever we need them. If you need to get away for a while, there are those buses to Pinecraft."

Rebecca tucked a strand of dark hair behind her ear. "Mem, will you let me talk for just a few minutes, please? I'm going to Oregon because I have a scholarship. I'm going to nursing school. I'm going to be a nurse."

"A nurse?" The disbelief and shock on Mem's face couldn't have been more apparent if Rebecca had told her that she was going to the moon.

"How in the world can you become a nurse?" Dat interjected. "They have requirements . . ."

"Requirements that I've met." Rebecca crossed her arms over her chest and pulled them in tight. She felt like shouting at her parents, telling them to listen to her. Anger swept in, heating her face. Over the last few days she'd felt guilty for leaving. But now, trying to have this conversation, she remembered why she'd chosen to do what she did.

"What do you mean you've met the requirements?"

Rebecca didn't know what to do but just confess everything. They were already angry, hurt . . . What more could she do to make them ache so? A lot, she realized, and that ache would come with her words.

"For the last three years I've been taking online classes. I've borrowed a computer, and I got my high school diploma. I had a friend who helped me with scholarships. She wrote letters for me, and most of my fees were waived because of my unique circumstances. People felt sorry for me because in the eyes of my family and community my desire for an education was considered to be going against the church." She looked into his eyes. "I have a diploma, Dat. I have an associate's degree, and I've also taken a few Emergency Medical Technician classes."

Where most *Englisch* parents would be proud, tears filled

her father's eyes. Getting schooling according to the ways of the world was no good to them. It meant becoming full of head knowledge. It meant walking in the ways of the world.

"And in Oregon . . . you're going to nursing school? You've already been accepted?" There was a tremble in Mem's voice. "That's not possible . . . You're an Amish woman, Rebecca. Your role is to join the church. To marry. To have children."

"That's what the role of most Amish wo—"

"Yours! It's yours." Mem raised her voice, and then the tears came harder and she covered her face with her hands, lowering it so all Rebecca could see was the top of her starched white *kapp*.

Rebecca did her best to keep her voice steady. How could she make them understand? "But what if I were to say that I feel called to this, Mem?" she said, barely above a whisper. "That I felt that God was going to do a good work with me? I've worked so hard, and God has brought help in unexpected ways. I feel that I am supposed to go to nursing school, and after that . . ." She paused there. As she spoke, Caleb's face flashed in her mind. Yes, she cared for him, but if God had plans for them to be together, He'd bring that about somehow, just as He'd brought them together. She didn't need to bring him up now. Not yet.

"Someday I might find a *gut* Amishman and marry and have children," she continued.

"A *gut* Amishman will not want a woman like you."

"I know you believe that." She lowered her head and looked to her lap. "That's a risk I'm willing to take."

"And when are you heading there? When are you going to Oregon?"

"Tomorrow." The answer came quickly, yet even as Rebecca said those words, she knew it was the right answer. She couldn't imagine going back on the wagon ride. She'd have more time with Caleb if she did, but that would just make things harder when she left. And then she'd also feel the tension of her parents being here. They wouldn't leave Montana until she did. She wouldn't be able to relax. She would have to face this battle day after day. No, it was best that she left as soon as possible.

"Is there anything that we can do to make you change your mind?"

"No, nothing."

"Tomorrow?" her mem asked again.

Rebecca remembered seeing on the Amtrak map that there was a station in Libby. She had her suitcase. She had everything she needed. She could go. "*Ja*."

Her heart ached at having to tell Caleb. Would he understand?

Rebecca stood. "I'm going to go talk to my friends and get my things. And if it's okay, can I stay with you here tonight? I'd like some time with you—"

"If that's what you want," her mother interrupted. "Are you sure your *Englisch* friends won't mind?"

"*Englisch* and Amish," she corrected. "Ike, Caleb, Amos . . . they are all Amish, and—"

"Anyone who would be such close friends with the *Englisch* might as well be *Englisch* themselves," Dat commented.

Rebecca nodded, but she didn't respond. It would be no use commenting. It would be no use trying to explain herself. Not even bringing up Claudia's death would help. If anything, it would make her parents focus on the fact they'd lost two daughters. Over the months to come she could pray for their understanding. She could pray that God would speak to their hearts. But until then she'd just have to live with the knowledge that she'd disappointed her parents.

"Would you like me to bring you back some food? Or maybe we could go to dinner. If you'd like to meet my friends."

"*Ne*, we'll be fine." Mem's voice was curt, and she looked weary with the realization that they'd come all this way and it had done no good.

When Rebecca walked outside, Marianna was still waiting in the truck.

"How did it go?" she asked as Rebecca climbed in.

"Not well. They don't understand at all."

"Did you think they would?"

"*Ne*, the truth is that what happened is exactly what I expected."

"So what's going to happen now?" Marianna asked.

"Tomorrow I'm getting on a train."

Marianna gasped. "What? Are you going back with them?"

"*Ne*, I'm heading to Oregon. I'm going to set out to do what I started."

"And what about Caleb? I could see the looks that have passed between you. Something special is there, Rebecca."

"*Ja*, and I just have to trust that God will show us a way."

CHAPTER

25

By the time they got back to the campsite, the horses were corralled and the tents were set up. Tears filled Rebecca's eyes to see her tent right next to Annie's. She had no doubt that her sleeping bag, pillow, and suitcase were inside.

The guys were sitting on a bench looking through a phone book. Ike looked up and waved as she and Marianna approached. "Now that we're in civilization, we're having a hard time deciding what to eat."

"Pizza!" Annie called from where she and Millie were playing horseshoes. "That's the only thing I can guarantee you won't be having on the trail."

As Rebecca approached, Caleb glanced up and smiled. Then his smile faded. Worry filled his face. He'd probably guessed that things hadn't gone well.

He stood and strode up to her, reached out and took her hand, rubbing her fingers. "Hey, are you okay?"

"*Ne*, not at all. They want me to go home with them. They don't understand. They believe I'm making a horrible choice. And . . ." She looked into his eyes. "They're ashamed of me—of what I've done. You can see it all over their faces."

"I'm so sorry, Rebecca. I know that you expected things would be like this, but that doesn't make the pain easier."

She nodded, knowing that what she had to tell him next would be even harder.

"As I talked to them, I had a feeling that I had to continue on—to stick to my plan. They need to know that I'm serious. They need to be able to return home and mourn, just as they had to do with Claudia."

"I'm sorry. I don't understand." He let go of her and crossed his arms.

"You're not going to like what I have to say, Caleb."

"I don't like the sound of that."

She turned away. "I need to leave. I'm not going to go on the wagon train back. I need to go on. I need to go to Portland."

"Excuse me?" His voice took on a sharp tone, even though she could tell he was trying to control it. "You're going to walk away from the only time we're going to have together for a while?"

She stretched her neck and lifted her chin. "I don't want you to think that I'm leaving you. That's not what I'm doing."

"You're letting them do this to you. You're running again." He took her arm and gently spun her back around to face him. "You said yourself that school doesn't start for a few weeks. I want you to think about my heart. I want this time with you."

"Please, Caleb. They aren't going to leave until I do."

"Then I'm going to follow you. I'll go to Portland for a few weeks. I can help you there."

"No." The word shot from her lips. Her eyes widened. "Do you know how that'll look?" She gazed into his blue eyes, telling herself to stay strong. "You'll be all right. We'll be all right." She reached up and placed a hand on his chest. His plaid shirt was warm from the sun, and she could feel the pounding of his heart from within. His heartbeat was quick, and from the look in his eyes, his mind raced just as quickly.

"I'll consider coming back at Thanksgiving or Christmas. It's only a day's ride on the train. It's not that far, and we can go for a hike in the snow."

She tried to forget that the others were no doubt watching them. She tried to ignore the wind chime that rang out again and again from the motor home parked just a few slots over. She told herself that this was the hard part—that once she got on the train everything would be all right. But that wasn't the truth either. Once one had given part of one's heart away, it would always ache—at least until it was reunited with the other half again.

"What if I said I wasn't going to be here? That maybe I'd already thought about leaving Montana?" Caleb said.

Their eyes met again. Now it was her turn to say, "Excuse me?"

"Oh, you don't like that, do you?" he huffed. "I was going to wait until you left in a few weeks, but I might go sooner."

"But why?" She brushed a few dark strands of hair back from her face.

"My *opa*. I thought you would have figured it out. You were right when you said that he would be happy to see me— that he wouldn't be bothered about the condition of his farm as much as he'd be happy to see me. I've been selfish, Rebecca. I told myself that I was only following the advice he gave me. That it was important for me to experience life and to see different parts of the world. That it would be important to him. But I was protecting myself. I didn't want to feel the ache of seeing him like that. I didn't want to see the shell of the man while longing for the bright, active *Opa* I used to know. But something Millie told me really helped."

"What's that, Caleb?"

"She told me that we think we're in the land of the living and then we die, but the opposite is true. We're in the land of the dying, and it's only after we die that we truly live. I need to be there for *Opa*."

"I think you're right, Caleb. I can't wait to hear about it when you go back. Do you promise to write and call?"

Caleb ran a finger down her cheek. "Of course, Rebecca. You're not going to get rid of me that easily."

Their last dinner together wasn't anything special, but Rebecca realized it was right. It was comfortable. And wasn't that how all good friendships—good relationships—should be?

They ate dinner at Young Gun's Pizza. Then, with Caleb in the backseat, Marianna drove her back to her parents' motel room. Her parents were still waiting up, and after she briefly introduced them to Caleb, they whisked her inside the hotel room door as if they were protecting her from an unseen foe. Caleb was still Amish, and Marianna had grown up Amish, yet they treated them as if they had tainted Rebecca. As if her being around them had changed her—something she couldn't deny.

Her last look at Caleb was a brief glance over her shoulder. He mouthed something, but she couldn't tell what. "I care" or "I'll call." Either way, she had hopes that he would still be in her life for a very long time.

Sometime in the night, Rebecca woke to a noise and a stuffy room. She could hear her father's snores in the next bed over and her mother's heavy breathing. The red, glowing numbers of the alarm clock read 2:32. It was dark outside and the wind had picked up.

It was only as the drone of low thunder rumbled again that she realized that's what had woken her from her dream. She'd been dreaming that she was already on the train and it was pulling out from the train station. The thought of it nearly broke her heart in two.

Her fingers touched her lips where Caleb had softly kissed her. Was it just yesterday? Grayish light filtered through the hotel room curtains, and she hoped the rain would stay away. She snuggled farther down into the sheets and blankets of the hotel room bed, wondering what it would be like to wake up and look into the face of someone you loved. Did Caleb wonder the same?

She wondered if they'd ever get the chance to find out.

CHAPTER

26

At nine o'clock there came a knock on the door. Rebecca and her parents had just gotten back from breakfast. Rebecca's heart leapt. Was it Caleb coming to say one last good-bye? She tried not to act disappointed when she saw that it was Marianna and Ben.

"Hi, what's happening? Is everything all right?" Rebecca asked.

"*Ja*, we just remembered something: you didn't make it to Kootenai Falls and the swinging bridge. It seems a shame that you went the whole way on the wagon trail and missed that."

"What about the others? Are they going?" Her heart skipped a beat.

Ben and Marianna exchanged looks. "They're already headed there in the wagons but won't be there for a few hours yet," Marianna explained. "We couldn't fit everyone in the truck, and, well . . . I suppose we could have brought Caleb, but I was being a little selfish and wanted this time just with you. Who knows when I'll see you again?"

Rebecca nodded, disappointment filling her. "*Ja*, that makes sense."

Ben and Marianna also invited her parents to join them on their short trip, but they both declined. Even though Rebecca and Marianna had grown up as friends—and it was impossible to count how many times Marianna had slept over at her house as a girl—Rebecca's mother treated her like a stranger.

Rebecca cast her parents a parting smile, thankful to be free of the tension that filled the hotel room. "I'll see you later, at the train station, for one last good-bye before the train ride. Are you sure you can get there okay?"

"*Ja*, we found the taxi ride here to the hotel, didn't we?" Dat said with an edginess to his voice.

"Have a nice time," Mem said with no emotion.

She had hurt them. But hopefully it was a hurt that time would heal.

Ben drove a ways out of town, and then he parked just off the highway near a small sign that read *Kootenai Falls and Swinging Bridge*. There were restrooms and a hiking trail with a sign that pointed the direction to the falls. Rebecca tried to listen for the falling water, but all she heard was the roaring of the passing trucks.

"Do you think our stuff will be okay here?" she asked as she climbed out of the truck. "That suitcase has everything I own in it." She tossed Millie's jacket haphazardly over the case so that it didn't look like anything important.

"Are you kidding? This is Montana," Ben said. "Most people don't lock their car doors, and I even have friends who don't put locks on the doors to their houses."

"*Ja, vell*, it's pretty safe back in LaGrange County, too, but things still happen."

"It's fine," Marianna commented, patting Rebecca's arm.

234

"It's a quick hike there and back. We can't take too long. We need to make sure you get lunch before you catch your afternoon train."

Rebecca nodded and followed them down the trail. It was well worn, and a few other tourists were coming and going. A man walking a dog offered her a hello as they passed and she smiled back. Ahead of her, Marianna slipped her small hand into Ben's larger one, and Rebecca's heart ached.

Even though she'd never seriously dated before, and even though she'd only known Caleb for a week, it seemed wrong to Rebecca that she was walking alone. She felt empty and anxious. It just didn't seem right not to have him by her side, and that worried her. How was she going to handle being in Portland alone? How was she going to get through it?

They walked through the woods and then found themselves at a large crossing that took them over railroad tracks. They climbed a set of steps, crossed over the tracks on a metal bridge, and then climbed back down again.

It was as they reached the other side that Rebecca heard the roaring of the falls. She thought of the waterfall she'd found with Caleb, and she was reminded of the way she'd tossed pinecones into the water, watching them swirl and tumble. She felt like that now, moving down a path that was going to wash her away, taking her from those she cared about.

As they entered the woods again, the walking trail teed. They went to the right first, and she noticed the falls. It wasn't a large, tall falls like she'd expected, but rather a series of wide steps that moved downward. The steps were so even and well designed they looked man-made. An older lady and man were sitting on the rocks on the side, enjoying the view. Marianna approached them.

"You wouldn't mind taking a photo of the three of us, would you?" she asked.

"Not at all." The man jumped to his feet and took the camera from Marianna's hands. Marianna motioned to Rebecca. "*Kumme.*"

Rebecca hurried to her side with the falls at their back. Ben walked over and stood behind them both, placing a hand on each of their shoulders. She forced a smile as she looked at the camera, guessing it was one of only a dozen photographs that had been taken of her over the years.

It's a new life, she thought to herself, unsure if that was a good thing.

When the picture was taken, they sat down on the rocks, and she let herself focus on the falls. They were there to remind her that if God created this place, He had a good plan for her life too.

"So, are we going to go to the swinging bridge?" Ben asked.

Marianna rubbed her stomach. "To tell you the truth, I've been laying around that house all week, and I'm feeling a little lazy. You don't mind taking Rebecca down to the bridge while I wait here, do you?"

"No. Wait." Rebecca rose and motioned for Ben to stay seated. "I don't mind going by myself. That sign said it's only a quarter mile down the river, along the trail, right?"

Ben nodded. "Yeah, something like that."

She took a few steps toward the trail "Yes, see. That'll only take me fifteen minutes there and back. You two just stay here, watch the falls. Or, better yet, stare into each other's eyes." Rebecca turned and headed to the trail before they could argue.

"Are you sure?" Marianna called to her.

"I'm fine!" Rebecca replied without looking back. She

needed this. She needed time to think, time to pray, before she got on that train.

Rebecca was the only one traveling down the trail. She could still hear the falls, and she could also make out the river through the trees every now and then. She walked around trees and up small rises and down again, and just when she thought she'd somehow missed the bridge, there it was.

It was a narrow hanging bridge, made of planks and rope. It was wide enough for only one person at a time to walk on, and it swooped down in the middle as it crossed the water. As she climbed up the stairs to get to it, she couldn't help but remember what Millie had said about Jesus being the bridge.

As she got closer, she noticed it was three planks wide, and a metal fence had been run down both sides and set onto posts. Rebecca took the first step and was amazed how shaky it was—not a firm foundation at all.

She walked to the middle of the bridge and couldn't help but think of the covered bridges back in Indiana—kissing bridges, as they were called. She'd always imagined herself growing up there, getting married there, growing old there. She'd imagined kissing her beau every time they passed under a kissing bridge. She had imagined living in the same church community as her parents and *aentis*. But life had a way of changing the rules. God had a way of changing one's plans.

She walked all the way across the bridge to the wooded area along the side. She took in the scent of pine and tried to remember how fresh the air could be—and how it filled her soul as well as her lungs.

She turned to head back across the bridge, picturing Caleb walking through those woods and greeting her. She held her breath, almost wishing it was so. But he wasn't there.

Yet God was.

A warm breeze hit her face, and even as she stood there, she knew that things would be all right.

Trust me, she felt God saying. *I will always be with you.*

Peace settled over her, and she felt braver about riding on the train, about heading to Portland. God had brought her this far. He'd done so much. Surely He wouldn't leave her now.

Her steps felt lighter as she exited the bridge and made her way back down the trail. By the time she got back to the falls, Ben and Marianna were already standing.

"There you are!" Ben called. "I was just going to come and check on you."

"I'm fine. Good, even." Rebecca smiled. "I was just back there on that bridge getting a pep talk from God."

Marianna came and wrapped her arm around Rebecca's shoulders. "I'm glad. And I'm thankful we had some time together. I know it's been a challenge, as we're both growing and changing, but I want you to know I consider you my forever friend."

"I feel the same." Rebecca thought about mentioning coming back for Thanksgiving, but it seemed foolish to try to plan for something so far away. The best way to follow God, she was discovering, was to focus ahead on where you hoped to be, but to be willing to make adjustments to those plans.

They exited the woods and then climbed up the metal stairs, crossing over the train bridge once again. A siren blared from somewhere, carrying through the trees.

When they got closer to the parking lot, Ben stopped short. "It sounds like somebody's car alarm is going off."

"I thought you said there isn't any crime in Montana." Rebecca smirked.

He shrugged and resumed his pace again. "I bet somebody set off their car alarm accidentally."

"It's not your truck, is it?" Rebecca asked.

Marianna shook her head. "I don't even think our truck has an alarm. Does it, Ben?"

"I think it does." He pulled out his keys from his pocket. "I'm not sure."

The alarm stopped.

"Did you push a button?" Marianna asked him.

"I didn't push anything. It must have been someone else's vehicle."

"Either someone turned off their alarm or its two minutes were up," Rebecca said.

Ben turned her direction. "What do you mean?"

"Those alarms—they only sound for two minutes. Then they turn off on their own. It saves the battery."

"And how do you know this? Aren't you Amish?" he chuckled.

"*Ja*, but I worked at a restaurant most of my teen years. I used to page many customers about their car alarms, until I learned they eventually turn off. In Shipshe, most of the time the car just got bumped. Of course, there were times when the cars had been broken into and things were stolen . . ." She let her voice trail off. "People loved taking items from tourists . . ."

My suitcase. What if someone broke in and took it? Worried thoughts pounded her, breaking through the peace she'd felt just a moment before.

Even though Ben didn't seem concerned, Rebecca quickened her pace. What if that had been Ben's truck's alarm? Her heart started pounding, and she told herself it was nothing. But the truth was that if anything happened to that suitcase, she was in trouble.

Rebecca went from walking to running. As she rounded

the corner to the parking lot, she stopped short. Ben's truck was just where they left it, but another car was parked next to it, and two women were peering into a broken window on Ben's truck.

"Stop! What are you doing?" she called to them, running up. She could hear Ben's footsteps pounding behind her.

"Is this your truck, sweetie? The alarm was going off when we parked and the window was broken. We thought we'd watch it until the owner arrived."

Rebecca nodded and moved past them, reaching for the door handle. "It's not my truck, but my things were inside!" Rebecca swung the passenger's-side door open and looked behind the seat. Tears immediately sprang to her eyes, and her knees softened.

Ben stopped in his tracks near the back of the truck. "I don't believe it." The tarp had been pulled off their camping items and was lying on the ground.

"They didn't get into the cab, did they?" Marianna hurried up. "My purse is in there. I tucked it under the front seat."

Rebecca clung to the truck's backseat, feeling as if her whole world was caving in. "My suitcase. It was in the backseat. It's gone." As she said those words the world around her turned to shades of gray. "Can you call the cops? We need to tell them—" she hurriedly asked.

"My purse is here!" Marianna's words interrupted her own. "For the first time I won't complain about all the junk Ben keeps in this rig. They didn't even see it."

"But my suitcase." Rebecca squatted to the ground and covered her face with her hands.

"I'm not sure what the cops can do." Ben approached. "This is a highway. Who knows who did this and where they are now."

Marianna came to her, placing her hand on Rebecca's shoulder. "I'm so sorry. I know your suitcase had your clothes . . . all your things that you were taking to Portland."

"It was more than that. It had everything I needed to live on!"

"There are a few shops in Libby, if you need clothes or other items." Marianna leaned down, trying to be supportive. "I know it'll be hard not to have your things, but Portland is big. I'm sure you can find whatever you need there. If you need to borrow some money to replace your things . . ." Marianna turned to Ben. "I'm sure we can help."

"Ten thousand dollars." Rebecca's tears came then. "My grandma had been saving it most of her life. One dollar from her eggs, here and there. Five dollars from pretty aprons she sewed. She worked so hard . . . and that's what I was going to live on. My scholarship only covered school. I have to pay for my apartment—my living expenses. What am I going to do? I can't get a job. I was worried about keeping up as it is just with schooling. The studies are going to take everything out of me. How am I going to be able to work? I—I can't do that." She sank all the way to the ground, sitting on her bottom, not caring that the ground was damp. Not caring about anything.

Is this what I get for walking away? I thought I was trying to do a good thing, God. Those people need help. So many need help . . . Why are You punishing me like this?

The silent prayer ripped through her soul, and she thought about Caleb. Was God going to take everything away from her? Wasn't it hard enough to leave all she knew? To try to make it in an *Englisch* world?

"Wait? Are you saying that you had ten thousand dollars in your suitcase?" Marianna looked down at her.

"*Ja.*"

Ben shook his head in disbelief. "Well, you should have said that before we left the truck."

She looked up at him. "I asked you if my things were going to be all right . . ."

"Yes, Rebecca, but I thought you meant your aprons and bonnets. I had no idea . . ."

From the corner of her eye, Rebecca noticed Marianna typing in something on her phone. Ben noticed it too.

"What are you doing?" he asked.

"I'm calling the police department. We have to report this."

"But what about making the train?" Ben asked.

"Without that money there's no use." Rebecca released a shuddering breath. "Without that money I'll have no choice but to return home to Indiana."

CHAPTER

27

Rebecca's fingers drummed on the desk, wanting to hide from the intense gaze of the officer's eyes.

"Are you telling me that you sewed ten *thousand* dollars into the lining of an old suitcase that you picked up at a thrift store? Haven't you ever heard of a bank account, miss? Are you trying to tell me you're *Amish*?"

Rebecca shrank back from the man's disbelieving stare.

"Sir, yes, I grew up Amish, and I was still wearing my Amish clothes up to a day ago. If you find my suitcase you'll discover the truth—all my Amish clothes are inside."

"Mm-hmm." He jotted down notes.

Was he going to do anything about it? Would he tell her that she was out of luck and usher her out?

She cocked her chin, feeling it was worthless talking to him, knowing all that she had was gone. "Sir, don't you know how we Amish do things? My mem saves all her money in jelly jars in the basement, *ja*? And all of that money came from my grandmother. From her chickens, actually. She sold their eggs and saved all the coins for years. She didn't trust banks, but if she was alive, I'd tell her that hiding money isn't so safe either."

Rebecca glanced at Marianna from the corner of her eye. Her friend's eyes grew wide. She guessed Marianna was trying to hold back a smile. It seemed that every time one got beyond Indiana, Ohio, or Pennsylvania, no one knew how to handle one's talk of being Amish.

The officer took more notes and nodded. Did he believe them at all?

Rebecca stopped her tapping and cleared her throat. "So, do you think there is any chance?"

"Well." He pushed his glasses down on the tip of his nose. "I have good news and bad news. The bad news is that because it was stolen from the highway, the thieves could be all the way to Idaho by now. The good news is that if the suitcase was in as bad of shape as you said, then they might have tossed it. I'll send out an APB for my guys to keep an eye out. Can I get the best number to contact you?"

Rebecca gave the officer the number to her cell phone, and Marianna's number as a backup. Ben then proceeded to tell them the other things that were stolen. A toolbox and a duffel bag with his clothes. No one had been interested in their camping gear.

When they finished, the cop escorted them outside. Rebecca felt as if her whole world had caved in. There was no use going to Oregon. She'd been counting on that money to pay for her housing and food and everything else she'd need over the next year. Even if she found a part-time job, she'd never be able to get her start.

As they walked through the parking lot to their truck, she thought about her parents. "So are we going back . . . to drop me off at the hotel to be with Mem and Dat?" she asked.

She watched her feet as she walked to the truck.

"No, Rebecca." Marianna's voice was sharp. "We're going

to run by the bank, and then we'll have just enough time for you to give them a quick good-bye before the train."

Rebecca paused her steps, glancing over at her friend. "Didn't you hear what I said?"

"I did. We did. Ben and I are going to pull some money from our savings. We can't give you the whole amount, but we can give you enough to replace your things and cover a few months of rent."

Rebecca placed a hand over her heart. "What? No . . . no, I can't accept that."

"Listen." Ben walked up to Rebecca. "I'm not sure if you've heard, but I recorded a song that did pretty well. Marianna and I set aside money from the proceeds to help people . . . and this is something we'd like to do."

"I can't accept that from you. It's too much."

Ben rubbed his brow. "It'll ease my conscience. Believe me, I'll be able to sleep better tonight, tomorrow night, if you take it. Besides, God's Word says, 'Give as freely as you have received.'"

"But . . . we need to hurry." Marianna pointed to the truck. "We have less than an hour to stop by the bank and say our good-byes. And pray." She smiled. "I wouldn't put it past God to do a miracle here."

Rebecca stood with Marianna on the platform. Marianna offered a too-bright smile. Rebecca's parents hadn't shown up as they'd said they would. Ben had run back to see if they'd needed a ride, but there was no answer at the door.

Marianna believed they had gone to lunch and had just lost track of time, but Rebecca felt otherwise. Mem was heartbroken, and she didn't want anyone to see her cry. The same had happened after Claudia's death. Instead of gathering her family together, Mem had turned away. She'd wallowed in her grief alone. Rebecca just hoped Mem turned to God in those times. No one deserved to be alone in her pain.

Ben approached and handed Rebecca the train ticket. "Here you go. Portland will meet you on the other side."

"*Danki.*" Rebecca nodded and tears welled up. Ben leaned forward and placed a hand on her shoulder. "Time'll go fast. You'll see. Then you can come back to Montana and have a second chance at spotting a bear."

"It's not the bear that eludes her." Marianna sighed. "She had her eye on something else—someone else."

The call to board sounded, and Marianna offered a hug, clinging tight.

"Take care of that *boppli*, will you?" Rebecca whispered in her ear.

Marianna stepped back and wiped away her tears. "*Ja*, of course."

"Do you mind if we say a ten-second prayer?" Ben asked.

"Of course not."

"Lord, be with my sister here. Watch over her. Show her favor. And we have faith, Lord, that you can even bring that suitcase back to her. Amen."

Rebecca patted her pocket with her new wallet, new toothbrush, and her cell phone. All she had left in this world. And then she turned and strode onto the train. She sank into the seat nearest the door, unable to go any farther. Marianna and Ben stood on the platform, the small white train station looking like something off a greeting card behind them. She tried not to feel jealous that Marianna had the picture-perfect life. And what did she have to look forward to? Eleven hours on the train with no one waiting on the other side. At least she could sleep.

Rebecca settled back into the seat, snuggling down the best she could and wishing that she had a blanket. The train started, picking up speed and clacking on the tracks. Just as she was dozing off, Rebecca's phone rang. She checked the number. It was from the hotel her parents had been staying at. Rebecca didn't have the energy to answer. She was dealing with her own questions; she didn't have enough energy to reach out to them, to apologize again.

Rebecca turned off her phone and settled back down. Tomorrow she'd call her parents back. Tomorrow she'd face her new life in Portland. Right now she was going to allow herself to fall asleep and dream about Caleb. Dream that they were walking in the woods, breathing in the fresh pine scent, and planning their life together.

CHAPTER

28

Rebecca hadn't realized how long she'd been sleeping until the conductor approached, shaking her shoulder.

"Weren't you getting off in Portland, miss? We're here."

Rebecca sat up and rubbed her eyes, sure that someone was playing a joke on her. But when she looked out, she saw a *Welcome to Portland, Union Station* sign on the building.

"*Danki*—thank you, sir." She checked to see if she still had her phone and wallet and then stepped off the train. She wasn't in a hurry as she walked to the station, and something above her caught her eye. Rebecca turned back and looked up. There, crossing from Union Station—over the train tracks— was a bridge.

A bridge! She gasped and pulled her phone from her pocket, snapping a photo.

"Do you like that, miss?" A baggage handler approached her.

"Yes, very much. Bridges have come to mean a lot to me these days."

"It's a pedestrian bridge. There's just an apartment complex on the other side, but you're welcome to go across. It'll give you a nice view of Bridgetown."

"Bridgetown?"

"Yes, didn't you know that was Portland's nickname?"

"No." Tears slid down her cheeks. She guessed the baggage clerk was going to worry about her, but she didn't care.

She wiped her tears away and then looked down at the photo she'd snapped on her phone. She could see a few pedestrians on the bridge and . . . Rebecca gasped. One of the pedestrians was looking down at the train, and it appeared as though he was wearing an Amish hat. Homesickness slogged through her heart in a way she didn't expect. She zoomed in on the photo. It was someone in an Amishman's hat, all right, but she couldn't see his face.

Rebecca looked back up, but there was no one on the bridge. She wiped more tears and turned toward the train station.

"Looking for someone, sweetie?" The woman's voice rang out as clear as could be.

"Millie!" Rebecca turned to see her standing there, white hair and wrinkled cheeks pushed up in a smile. Millie wore a blue shirt and jeans. Her thumbs were hooked in the belt loops, but she released them and opened her arms.

"I'm sorry, but that good-bye in Montana was for the birds." Millie gave Rebecca a quick hug. "More than that, we have something to show you. An answer to prayer. He went to get it from my truck."

"He?" Rebecca turned the direction Millie was pointing, and her heart felt as if it was going to jump out of her chest from all its wild beating.

"He . . . Caleb. That's who." Millie pointed, but Rebecca didn't need her help finding him in the crowd. She saw him, in his Amish pants, shirt, and suspenders, striding toward her. His smile was wide. His eyes were bright. And in her hand was a suitcase. Her suitcase!

"How in the world? What . . . How did you get it?"

"A trooper found it on the side of the road. It seems whoever stole it took out all your stuff . . . and tossed the suitcase on the side. I suppose they thought it too tattered to be of any use."

"And did they find the . . ." She paused, wondering if Millie knew.

"The money?" Caleb asked.

"*Ja*, how did you know?"

"Marianna told us," Millie explained. "We tried to call your cell phone, but you didn't answer."

Rebecca shrugged, glancing bashfully up at Caleb. "I had a lot on my mind. I turned it off."

"Yes, well, we checked, and the money is there . . . along with your written prayers." Millie chuckled. "Instead of a God box, I see that you have a God suitcase. I think that works just fine. Plenty of room."

"But how did you get here before me?" Rebecca asked. "Last I heard you were on your way to the falls."

"They found the suitcase about an hour after you left," Millie explained. "They got ahold of Ben and Marianna, and they found us and gave us their truck to drive. Annie and Ike were going to come, but he convinced her to stay back and go on a date instead. And poor Amos got left watching over all our things—our wagons and horses." Millie cocked one eyebrow. "The train takes eleven hours, and it was eight hours and eight minutes to drive . . . exactly. We've been here an hour or so."

Rebecca chuckled. "So you've been waiting around?"

Caleb stepped forward and offered her a warm smile. "Just a little bit, but it was worth it. And we were able to enjoy the best clam chowder I've ever eaten."

"*Ach*, are you going to show me?"

Caleb offered his arm. "I have a lot to share about Portland, and we even have a chaperone."

Millie waved a hand. "Don't mind me!"

"Well, how long do you have to show me around?" she asked.

Caleb turned to her and poked out his bottom lip. "I'm sad to say, only one full day. I have reservations to catch a plane back to Ohio the day after next."

"A plane?" Rebecca placed her hands on her hips. "Really?"

"I had to be able to tell the story of the trip to my *opa*, didn't I? He always wanted to get up in a plane. Besides, that's the fastest way back to him."

"Ready for some clam chowder?" Millie said. "And then if you're up to it, we're going to do some serious retail therapy."

"Millie, that sounds fun, but I only have to replace my things in my suitcase. I'm fine, now that I have *Oma*'s money."

"Not to your friends. Everyone pitched in and sent me with a wad of cash." Millie wrapped an arm around Rebecca's shoulders. "We want to bless you, honey. We want to let you know that we believe in you . . . believe in all you're doing."

Rebecca swallowed hard and glanced up at the bridge. "*Danki.*" It was only a whisper but it came from her heart . . . way down deep in her heart.

Caleb walked along the cement sidewalk—a new addition since he'd been home. Last time he'd been there his grandfather was propped up in his hospital bed. The curtains had been drawn and the room had been shut tight. The air inside had smelled like a hospital.

Caleb's heart had ached, realizing that if he'd been well, *Opa* would have walked into a room like that and opened the drapes and the door wide. Yet when Caleb had left, *Opa* couldn't even lift his head, let alone open the window to the sunshine outside.

But today, not only the window was open wide, but the door was too. Caleb quickened his pace and stepped through the doorway.

"Ab–out time . . ." The slurred words met him as he entered. Caleb's head lifted and his eyes moved across the room to the figure in the bed. *Opa* was propped up on pillows, and his eyes were focused on Caleb.

"You—" Caleb removed his hat and tossed it on the hook, not knowing what to say, what to do. "You're talking?"

He rushed toward his grandfather. His mem was sitting at *Opa*'s side. Her face was lit in a smile.

"*Opa*, you're right. I'm so sorry it took me so long to come back." Then he turned to his mem. "How is this possible?"

"Did you know Mrs. Kelly down the street? Her daughter is a therapist. She's been coming to work with *Opa* for about an hour each day. I wrote about it in some of my letters . . ."

"Pretty?" The word slurred from *Opa*'s lips.

"Oh, Mrs. Kelly's daughter is pretty, is she?"

Opa gave the slightest furrowing of his brow. "*Ne.* Reb—Re . . ."

"Amos wrote us a letter," Mem explained. "*Opa* knows about Rebecca."

Caleb blushed but held his gaze steady on his grandfather's eyes. "*Ja.*" He nodded wildly. "Wouldn't have stayed away so long if she wasn't."

"Kiss?" *Opa* offered a half grin.

"My, you have become nosy. In spite of what you may think, I'm not one to share that type of information unless I have permission. But you can ask Rebecca when she comes."

"She's coming to Ohio?" Mem asked, clasping her hands together.

Caleb nodded. "I'm trying to talk her into coming for Christmas, if not sooner."

Caleb didn't mention nursing school. From the eagerness in Mem's eyes, he could tell Amos hadn't told Mem where Rebecca was . . . or about nursing school either. But there would be plenty of time to talk about that. To explain.

Instead Caleb sat down on *Opa*'s bed. "Do you forgive me, Grandfather?"

A shaky hand reached over and grabbed his.

"*Ja* . . ." His *opa*'s single word rang out clear.

That was all Caleb needed. His heart leapt. He could tell from his grandfather's face that all that mattered was that Caleb was there. Now all he needed to do was to figure out how to bring the woman he loved here too.

CHAPTER

29

FOUR MONTHS LATER

The small kitchen table sat covered with books. Rebecca's head hurt from studying, but it was better than the alternative. When she wasn't studying she was thinking, and when she was thinking she always thought of Caleb. Had she made a big mistake by coming here instead of going with him to Ohio? One could always follow one's dream, but how often did true love come one's way?

She slammed shut her nursing ethics book and rubbed her eyes, wondering if she'd still be able to fall asleep tonight if she took a nap now. There was nothing worse than being up at night tossing and turning.

Rebecca rose and slipped on her tennis shoes and pink hoodie. She decided to go for a walk instead. Or maybe she'd take the tram up to University Hospital and take in the view of the city, of the bridges.

She'd just finished zipping up her jacket and grabbing her apartment keys when a knock came at the door. Without hesitation she cupped her hands around her mouth. "Jennifer moved upstairs to apartment 214!" she called.

There was a reason the landlord had given her a discount on her apartment rent, she decided, and it had nothing to do with her sweet face. The former tenant was the most popular girl in Portland, and friends and suitors came by at all hours of the day—and sometimes night—to visit.

"I'm sorry. I don't know who Jennifer is, but your voice sounds like someone I've come a long way to see," the voice called back. She recognized that voice. She stood there. Her feet refused to move. Her stomach flipped and her heart pounded.

There was a second, softer knock. "Rebecca, are you going to let me in?"

Rebecca dropped her apartment keys and then quickly bent over to pick them up. She rushed to the door and swung it open. "Caleb, what in the world are you doing here?" Her emotion caught in her throat, and she felt like pinching herself. He was real. He was here. And he was even handsomer than she remembered.

A long moment passed and he seemed to be soaking in the sight of her too. His eyes filled with unanswered questions. "So, it's okay, then, that I showed up, *ja*?"

"Yes, of course! I've . . . I've been wanting to see you. I received your letters, and I'm sorry I haven't written back very often. It's just these studies are taking so much time . . ."

He stepped forward and looked down at her, his gaze tender. "I'm not a patient man."

"I know, but I'm thankful for the time that you gave me to think. I needed it. I needed it to know how much I miss you. How much I want you in my life." Tears filled her eyes.

"I was hoping you'd say that, Rebecca. Or at least something close." Without another word, he bent to her and ran a finger down her jawline. Rebecca's heart quickened its beat and threatened to burst from her chest. She dropped her hands to her sides, telling herself not to leap into his arms. Telling herself to let him take the lead.

"How . . . how long are you going to be here?"

He stepped in, closer. "I haven't decided yet, but I don't think we should waste any time."

Rebecca told herself to breathe. She tried to blink back her happy tears, but it was no use.

He touched his thumb to her face, wiping away a stray tear. "Hey, you look a little stressed." He leaned closer, closer. Rebecca lifted her chin to him. She'd been thinking of this— their first real kiss—but just before his lips touched hers, Caleb pulled back.

"I was, uh, stressed until now." She blew out a breath, again amazed by how such a strong guy could be so tender and compassionate too. Amazed by his self-control. *It's all right, just kiss me,* she wanted to tell him.

But instead of leaning in, he wiped her tears again and then stepped back. "I have a surprise for you, if you're up for it."

"Why wouldn't I be? But I have to do this first . . ." Abandoning her earlier reserve, she rose up on tiptoe. Her arms circled his shoulders. She clung to him, offering him a hug.

She couldn't believe that after all these months he was here. There were many nights that she'd lain awake wondering if he'd just been a dream. Or at least wondering if she'd put more stock into the idea of a relationship than he had. Even though he'd written her faithfully, she'd worried that she had her hopes up for no reason. Yet he'd come! Caleb had come all this way to see her. She released her hug and pulled back. His eyes were fixed on hers, and then he looked to her lips. It was clear that he wanted to kiss her . . . but why wasn't he?

He offered her another smile, stepped back, and motioned for her to follow. She locked her apartment and then followed him to the parking lot, scanning it for a car and driver. Nothing. She glanced at her watch, realizing the next city bus wouldn't be there for another twenty minutes.

"Are we going to walk?" she asked.

"Why walk when we can use some horsepower? Motor power."

"You're driving?"

Caleb nodded and reached into his front jacket pocket, pulling out a wallet. He opened it and then slipped out a small, white, laminated card, handing it to her. "I'm a licensed driver."

It was an Ohio license with *motorcycle* written near his picture.

"How did you get this?" she asked. "Did you drive a motorcycle all the way here?"

"I started studying and practicing about a week after I got back to Ohio. I passed with flying colors." He cleared his throat. "And yes, I rode my motorcycle the whole way. It was quite the adventure. A full 2,510 miles and thirty-seven hours on the road . . . but who's counting?"

"And they took your photograph?" She waved his driver's license in the air. "If yer dat and mem saw this, Caleb, they'd faint straightaway and cry over how you'd lost your soul."

He chuckled as he approached a motorcycle that was parked near the front. "*Ja*, but if that is the case, then you'll have to go before the church with me and confess that you rode right behind me with your arms wrapped around tight." He pointed to the helmets on the handlebars.

"You're kidding, right?"

"What do you mean?" he asked. "We haven't been baptized into the church yet. They're not going to make us confess."

"Not that. Didn't you hear the story of how Annie's husband died on a *motorcycle*? Do you know the statistics of how many motorcycle accidents there are?"

Caleb crossed his arms over his chest. "No, I didn't learn that in Amish school. Go ahead . . ."

She bit her lower lip. "*Vell*, I'm not sure, but I know it's a lot."

He didn't budge. Instead he took a helmet from the handlebars and placed it on his head. "So are you saying that you're not going to see what I've planned for our day?" He handed the second helmet to her.

Rebecca sighed. "You're not going to give me a choice, are you?"

"We could walk, but that would mean getting there tomorrow, if we're lucky."

Rebecca sucked in a big breath. "If that's how things are going to be . . ." She took three tentative steps toward him.

"One thing's for certain, Rebecca: falling in love with me, your life will never be boring."

Once settled on the bike, they drove for at least twenty minutes. Rebecca's arms were wrapped tightly around Caleb's waist. She enjoyed watching over his shoulder, but she also enjoyed resting her cheek on his back. The wind was picking up, and a misty rain started falling. Rebecca's heart pounded, and she tried to forget that Caleb was a new driver and that she was most likely his first passenger. If she was going to allow herself to be close to him, then she would be risking everything over and over again.

More than once Caleb stopped too abruptly, but each time he righted them and the bike steadied itself. They drove into a more rural area that she hadn't been to before, and when the motorcycle began to slow, she peered over his shoulder. They were on a two-lane road lined with trees, and . . .

If she didn't see it, she wouldn't have believed it. There, in the middle of Portland, it appeared they'd been transported back to Indiana. There was a covered bridge! It was made of dark wood and the sides were opened. Guard rails protected the railings, and the sign on the bridge read *Cedar Crossing.*

Caleb parked the motorcycle, and she climbed off and then pulled off her helmet. Caleb did the same, and his smile caused his face to glow. He took her helmet and placed both of them on the handlebars.

"This is amazing. I can't believe this. A covered bridge in Portland!" She turned and wrapped her arms around Caleb's neck, unable to contain herself.

He leaned toward her ear, as if he was going to tell her a secret, and then he turned his head quickly and placed a soft kiss on her cheek. Rebecca fingered the button on his *Englisch* shirt. "It's about time." She sighed and smiled up at him. "But for this to be a kissing bridge, maybe we should actually be standing on the *bridge?*"

"Actually, that was just for starters." He took her hand and then led her onto the bridge. They'd barely made it ten feet under the covered roof when he paused, pulled her to him, bent down, and kissed her full on her lips. Butterflies danced in her stomach, and it felt as if a rushing heat moved through her limbs.

Caleb pulled back and gazed into her eyes. "Now that was worth driving 2,510 miles for."

She chuckled, still not believing that he'd found this for her . . . and had done this for her. She opened her mouth to thank him again when the sound of children's laughter filled her ears.

Two boys rode down the road on their bicycles. They paused when they saw the motorcycle and jumped off their bikes, eyeing it. Rebecca was about to call to them, telling them not to touch the motorcycle lest it fall over and hurt them, when they moved farther off the roadway and each picked up handfuls of rocks and hurried up to the bridge.

"Winner has to do the other's math homework!"

She tried to focus on Caleb's face, tried to keep her mind centered on him, but she couldn't get her thoughts off of Claude. The boys reminded her of her young brother. He'd done such a good job at writing her, and she'd done her best to write back in a timely manner. From his letters it was apparent her mother hadn't told him where Rebecca was or what she was doing. Yet she figured he'd find out soon enough. It was hard to keep things secret in a community like that.

"I want to talk to you." Caleb wrapped an arm around her waist. "I've been thinking about our future."

"*Ja*, well, I'm excited to hear, but I can't believe that you'd do this—you've given up hunting season to come visit me here."

"Don't you know that I've already found what I'm hunting for? You're better than any prize buck."

Rebecca playfully slugged his arm. "And I suppose that's a compliment?"

"I can beat ya!" A boy's voice rang out. Glancing back, Rebecca saw that they were having a contest to see who could throw the farthest.

"No, there's no way you can win." The redheaded boy's voice rose. He planted his foot on the bottom of the bridge's railing to give him a boost up.

"Hey, that's not fair!" The blond boy stamped his foot. "It's not winning if you stand on the bridge."

The redheaded boy stuck out his tongue. "Who says? I can stand on the bridge if I want. You're still not going to win."

"No, you can't win if yer cheating! Fine . . ." The blond boy jutted out his chin. "I'll climb up!"

The boy, who couldn't have been much older than nine or ten years, reached for the top railing and planted his foot, hoisting himself up.

"Hey, wait!" Caleb took a step away from Rebecca. "I don't think that's very safe."

The boy glanced back, but just briefly. Caleb took a few more steps. "Did you hear me?"

"I'm going to win for sure if I throw it from up here," said the blond boy.

"You better listen," Rebecca called. "You'd better get down."

Caleb moved toward the boy, but he paid him no mind. Instead he pulled a rock from his pocket and pulled his hand back. "This one will win for sure!"

The boy moved in slow motion—or maybe it just looked that way as Caleb raced to him. Upon the release of the rock, the boy's body continued forward . . . forward . . . His eyes widened as he overbalanced and he reached for the bridge railing.

All he caught was air.

"Tyson! Stop!" the redheaded boy called, but it did no good.

Tyson's foot caught on the railing as he was going over. With a *thunk*, his body hit the bridge support. A cry filled the air, and it was only as she was running toward the bridge railing that Rebecca realized it was her voice, her cry.

"Dear Lord, help him!" The words emerged from her lips without her thinking about them. Her feet seemed to be weighed down by concrete as she rushed to the railing. She looked over the railing. There, in the greenish-blue water, the boy struggled.

"Caleb!" She called his name, then turned to see he was already racing off the bridge and sprinting down the grassy embankment.

"Please, Lord, help Caleb to get to the boy in time!"

"Go! Call 911!" she shouted to the boy who was watching.

"See that house over there?" She pointed to the nearest house. "Call them. Pound on the door. Get help coming!"

The redheaded boy turned and sprinted to the house. It was only then that Rebecca turned her attention back to Caleb.

The blond boy still struggled in the water, but the current pulled him downstream. Without hesitation she raced off the bridge and onto the grassy embankment. If Caleb managed to get the boy out of the water, she needed to be there to help.

Caleb reached the spot that was parallel to the boy. No longer able to hold his head up, he was sinking. His body turned so he was facedown.

"Dear God, no!"

Even as her feet carried her down the slippery, grassy hillside, Rebecca kept her eyes on Caleb. She expected Caleb to jump into the water and swim to the boy. Instead he kept on running.

It was then that she saw it. Up ahead a tree grew out over the water instead of upward. Most of its branches hung low, but the boy was still as he floated toward them. *Wake up! Reach up!*

With quickened steps, Caleb ran down the log as easily as if he was running on pavement. Then, when he got to the end, he dove into the water. He hit with a splash and then emerged. Ten seconds later the boy's body reached him. Caleb hooked his arm under the boy's armpit and wrapped his arm around the boy's chest. The boy's head lifted out of the water, but he wasn't breathing. Caleb swam with one arm, pulling the boy along, and when he got to the shore Rebecca was there, waiting.

"He's not breathing." Caleb struggled for breath. He lifted the boy with his arms and carried him to her. Gingerly, he laid the boy down on the ground.

She did a quick assessment. It had been the boy's shoulder that had hit the railing. His shirt was torn and blood oozed out of the gash. "Caleb, can you take off your shirt and put pressure on that spot, please?"

Without hesitation he did it—taking off his outer shirt but leaving his white T-shirt clinging to his body. He pressed it against the wound.

With gentle fingers she checked the boy's neck. It seemed fine. She looked into his mouth and throat, making sure the airway was clear.

As gently as she could, Rebecca tilted the boy's head back, opening his airway. She leaned down and gave five quick breaths. The boy's chest rose slightly, but not enough. In the background she heard a siren wail. *Danki* . . .

She watched for breathing, but didn't see it. She placed the heel of her hand on the boy's breastbone. She placed her second hand on the first and pressed down. His body had more give than the plastic dummy she'd practiced on more times than she could count. "One, two, three, four, five . . ."

After chest compressions, she moved again to his breathing and gave two quick breaths. She knew from her classes that rescue breaths weren't as important as the chest compressions, and she moved back to them. From somewhere she could hear voices, and she guessed that a crowd was gathering.

Caleb stood and moved up the embankment. "Tell those cars to move," he called up toward the spectators on the bridge. "There's an ambulance coming!"

Rebecca wasn't sure how many minutes had passed. Five? More? The siren stopped and she could hear the footsteps of the EMTs.

"Ma'am, we'll take this from here."

They continued CPR. Rebecca watched. Her hands were in fists, willing the boy to live. To not give up. The EMTs did two more sets of chest compressions and breathing, and then they paused as one man checked his vitals. A look of relief came over him. "There's a pulse."

Caleb quickly filled them in on what had happened, and she watched as the medics secured the boy's neck and transferred him to a body board.

"He's not out of the woods yet, but it would be a different story if you two hadn't been here," one medic told the other as they carried him up the hill.

"You did a good job, ma'am," they said as they carried him away. "A fine job, both of you."

"The boy's mother is here," she heard someone call. Rebecca looked up and saw a woman in a yellow T-shirt and jeans running to the ambulance. The redheaded boy was with her. Tears streamed down her face, followed by cries of joy when she saw her son. The EMTs put the stretcher into the back of the ambulance. The woman climbed in. Less than a minute later it was driving away.

It was only then that Rebecca turned to Caleb. "Do you think we should follow him . . . to make sure he's okay?"

Caleb nodded, and then he reached for her. His body was wet, cold, but as she fell into his embrace, she realized that she was already trembling.

"Yes, we should go check on him, but I want you to know, Rebecca, that I'm proud of you. If you ever had a doubt that you were doing the right thing, remember this moment. Remember that boy."

CHAPTER

30

It took them awhile to find the right hospital. They visited two others, but no one would give them information. They knew they'd found the right one when they walked through the emergency room doors and a woman—the boy's mom—rushed toward them.

"I can't tell you how thankful I am. How grateful that you were there." The woman's words released in a breath. "Aiden, Tyson's friend, told us how you told him to get down, but he didn't listen. I'm just glad that you were there to help him."

Tyson. Rebecca already knew she'd never forget that name after hearing Aiden call it over and over as his friend tumbled into the water.

The woman placed a hand on Caleb's arm. "I'm just so glad that you were there to pull him out of the water. Aiden said that you looked like Superman the way you flew off that branch into the water. He'd been going for help, but he paused and looked back, spotting you."

Caleb ran a hand down his face. "Now, I don't know about that, yet, but I'm glad I could help. And it was Rebecca here who did the breathing and stuff—the CPR."

The woman turned to Rebecca and took her hands into her own. "Thank you. If it wasn't for you, then this would be the worst day of my life."

Rebecca squeezed the woman's hands. "So he's okay, then?"

"Oh yes, he's going to be fine. He's breathing on his own, and he was awake for a few minutes. I would invite you back to see him, but the doctor is stitching up that nasty gash in his shoulder. I faint at the sight of blood, so I'm opting out of that one." She gave a sad chuckle. "And then there are X-rays to check for any fractures." The woman blew out a slow breath. "And I thought it was going to be an uneventful night eating TV dinners and watching *Dancing with the Stars*."

"Everything changes so quickly," Rebecca said. "It's amazing how that can happen."

"Would you like to stay and see him? I mean, after he gets all taken care of. I'm not sure how long it will take, but you're welcome to."

"Actually, I don't think that's necessary." Rebecca released the woman's hands and looked to Caleb. "I think we've done our part. I'm just so thankful we were there. It's good to know that Tyson will be all right. Will you let him know we'll be praying for him?"

"Yes, yes, of course."

"And we won't keep you," Caleb said. "But I think we will sit over here in the waiting room and warm up." He glanced down at his clothes, which were still damp.

"Oh, look at you . . . ," the woman said. "Hold on one minute." She rushed over to the nurses' station and returned less than a minute later with two blankets.

"One for each of you," she said. "I told them you were the rescuers. The nurses were more than happy to offer warm blankets."

"That's wonderful." Rebecca took them, and then she motioned toward a plastic chair for Caleb to sit. She gave the woman a quick hug, and then Tyson's mother hurriedly returned to his side.

Rebecca wrapped one blanket around Caleb's shoulders and then did the same with hers. "I'm not wet—well, not completely—but that motorcycle isn't a warm ride."

"I don't blame you if you want to steal my blanket." Caleb winked.

"And I won't blame you for not finishing your speech . . . or whatever you were going to do on that bridge."

"*Ach*, that." Caleb brushed his hair back from his eyes and smiled. "I bet you'd like to know." He glanced around. "Well, this isn't exactly how I pictured spilling my heart, Rebecca. But if you don't mind, I at least have to start. I've . . . had a few things on my mind that I've wanted to tell you." And he settled back in the chair.

Rebecca thought Caleb looked out of place sitting in the hard plastic hospital chair. Although the blanket covered his shoulders, his Amish pants were muddy and still damp from jumping into the river. He wore his wet, muddy boots even though she'd urged him to take them off so they could dry. Overhead a doctor was being paged, and next to them the elevator dinged and opened, offering up another passenger every few minutes.

Yet Caleb's attention wasn't on the chair, the pages, or even the elevator. His attention was fixed solely on her. She wanted to shrink back, to look away, but she forced herself to keep looking, to keep caring, and to not shield her heart.

"I traveled to Montana wanting adventure, and instead

I found a best friend. I can't imagine life apart from you, Rebecca. Whether here or there, I want us to be together. I . . ." He paused, looked intently at her.

"Can you just say it, Caleb?" She placed a hand over her pounding heart. "I know all the warning signs of cardiac arrest." She glanced at the watch on her wrist. "And I'm pretty sure I'm going to have a heart attack in the next thirty seconds if you don't just spit out the words. At least I'm in the right place if that happens. Unless you don't think you can . . . say them." She tilted her chin upward.

"Is that a challenge?"

"*Ja*, if you need it to be."

With a nod, he stood, took her hand, and then pulled her into a standing position. "There's no sitting down for this announcement." He chuckled.

She shifted her weight from side to side, waiting for his words.

"I love you, Rebecca."

She dove against him, and he wrapped his arms around her and lifted, just as she'd seen him do with the logs up in the mountains. But instead of tossing her, he held her close, tight. Tight enough that she couldn't get a full breath, which she guessed was only part of the reason she was light-headed.

She giggled. "I know everything will work out. Even though my mind is full of a thousand questions and I feel like a pine-cone being carried down a stream, I know everything will work out," she whispered in his ear, nuzzling her face into his neck.

"Don't let me off that easy." Caleb gently lowered her to the ground. Her toes touched first, and then her feet. "There's something more I have to say."

She tilted her head and studied his eyes, waiting.

"I tried to be brave, because it hides the fact that I'm so

scared at times. There are always these worries and doubts in my mind, but as things have played out . . . well, it's given me confidence that God has a perfect plan."

"What do you mean?" she asked.

"Think about Tyson. We just happened to be there. If traffic had been more backed up, we could have been sitting in a traffic jam. But we were there. Not only that. If you hadn't been there . . . Well, you knew exactly what to do. Without you he wouldn't have made it."

"And you," she quickly added. "No one else could have gotten to him in time."

Caleb nodded. "And I can't tell you the number of times people disapproved of me swimmin' when I should have been working."

"God knew, Caleb. Maybe He put that in you—your crazy need to run up trees and risk breaking your neck—to save one boy. It's strange to think of that, isn't it?"

"There's something else too." A shadow passed over Caleb's gaze. He opened his mouth and then closed it again. She could tell from his words that whatever was on his mind, it was hard for him to say.

"There was something that's always been hard for me to understand. The thought of one man's death changing so much. Jesus had to face it. He had to die, and yet because of that I'm different all these years later. Death changes us. The process of dying too. My grandfather's stroke changed me. And your sister's death . . ."

"*Ja*, I don't know where I would be if she were still around. Back in Indiana, I suppose. I'm not sure if I'd still be planning to stay Amish, but I wouldn't be here, that's for certain."

"More than that, Rebecca. If Claudia hadn't died the way she did, if you hadn't felt so helpless, we'd never be in Portland."

He sighed. "Yet because she died, Tyson has another chance at life. And after you finish school . . . who knows how many lives you will save."

The tears came now. Tears she couldn't hold back. "One life for many." And then a gasp escaped her lips. "I just remembered something. Something I hadn't thought about for a while."

"What's that?"

"Claudia was losing so much blood. She was getting weaker, yet there was this peaceful look on her face. She looked at her son and smiled, and then she looked to me. With the last of her strength she squeezed my hand. Her lips moved, and so I leaned down close. She whispered something. For so long I didn't understand . . ."

Rebecca's hands covered her face and a sob emerged, shaking her body. She cried, and Caleb held her. She knew then she could trust him. Trust he'd always be there to hold her. She also trusted more than she ever had that she was doing what God asked of her. She was leaving, but just for a season, and when she returned she'd be able to offer to her community what her sister never had.

"Claudia whispered, 'He knows what He's doing.' I thought she meant Claude, as he snuggled up to her breast, but she didn't mean that at all. She meant God. God had given her son life, but He was also asking for hers. God knew what He was doing. He knew . . ."

Caleb led her back to their chairs and blankets. An older couple entered with worried looks on their faces. Seeing Rebecca's tears, the woman pulled a small package of Kleenex from her purse and handed it to Rebecca.

"Thank you."

The older couple sat across the waiting room. They most

likely assumed Rebecca had just received horrible news. But the opposite was true. She'd never felt more at peace. She'd never felt more in love—not only with the man sitting next to her, but with God.

Caleb wrapped his arm around her, and in her soul Rebecca knew that things weren't going to be easy on the road ahead. There would be indescribably beautiful vistas, but also challenges, hardships, and fears that would meet them along the way. But they would make it, with God.

Caleb sat back and held her hands, resting them on the plastic armrest of the waiting room chair, rubbing her knuckles with his thumbs.

"Why don't we check on Tyson one more time and then head out?"

"That's a great idea. Then maybe after we get cleaned up we can head back to the bridge. I—well, things didn't turn out exactly as I planned. I mean, I'm not bitter . . . just anxious."

Rebecca rose. "*Ja*. Let's do it. My day is yours . . ."

He squeezed her arm. "I'll take it, Rebecca. I'll take all that I can get."

CHAPTER

31

Rebecca climbed off the back of the motorcycle, her heart pounding. The sun was setting, and it cast a golden glow over the bridge. Caleb got off and pulled off his helmet. His hair stuck up at all angles. She thought about brushing it down for him but changed her mind. It was Caleb, and he would always be a little wild.

His eyes lit on hers, and he brushed a few strands of hair back from her cheek, a soft smile on his lips. They walked under the covering of the bridge, and she stopped just as the asphalt turned to wood. He turned to her. Their gazes met and riveted.

"Don't move." Her voice was hardly more than a whisper. "I want to remember this moment. I'm burning it into my memory for good."

"Or you could take a picture." He pointed to her purse.

She chuckled and then pulled out her cell phone, snapping a picture. Viewing it, she glanced up at him. "There, now I'll be certain not to forget."

From his jacket pocket, he pulled out something. It was a pinecone. A small one just like she'd found in the woods of the Kootenai forest. "*Es dutt mir leed.* It got smashed."

"No need to be sorry." She glanced at him with a quavery smile. "You crazy, thoughtful, dreamy man." She blew out a quick breath. "Honestly, Caleb, I've never met anyone like you."

Rebecca took the pinecone from him and then allowed him to wrap his hand around hers. Caleb led her to the center of the bridge, where he leaned his hip against the side railing and motioned for her to step closer.

"I have something to ask you, but I want to talk to you first."

"*Ja*, already . . . but you're scaring me."

Caleb cleared his throat. "Nah, don't be scared. It's all *gut*. At least I think it will be. Rebecca, first I have to tell you that you're the reason I returned to Ohio. I was so focused on all the ways I was failing. I felt weak. I didn't think I could manage things as my *opa* did, and I felt everyone expected that from me. Instead of trying, I ran. I tried to push 'home' out of my mind, but it was impossible. How can a man walk away from his heart?

"I was so caught up on how things used to be that I wasn't thinking straight on what I was missing: time with my grandfather."

"What was it like when you went back?" Rebecca asked. He'd told her some in his letters, but she wanted to hear it from him face-to-face.

"*Gut*. We've had some long talks. Well, I talked a lot, but he was able to communicate some." Tears filled Caleb's eyes. "I'd been so concerned about not feeling like I measured up that I hadn't taken time just to look into my *opa*'s face. If I would have paused long enough and sat beside him on that porch, I would have *seen* what my heart had been wondering about. I would have seen that he loved me for me, not what I can do. He did like being on that porch—not so he could judge my efforts, but instead to just watch me, because he loved me."

Rebecca couldn't stop the tears, and it made her miss her own family in ways she couldn't describe. Should she write a letter to her family? Just to remind them again that she was all right, that she did want to return someday, and that she still loved them?

"I have something else I want to talk to you about too." Caleb cleared his throat. "Did you know, Rebecca, there's a department of nursing at a university in Canton? It's only thirty miles from my parents' house by car."

"In Ohio? Are you talking about Ohio? But what would your parents think about that? Surely they wouldn't approve."

"I was thinking if you continued nursing school there . . . we could get married." He reached up and touched her cheek. "And yes, Rebecca, that is what I was going to ask. I'm sorry I'm not more romantic."

She tried to wrap her mind around what he was saying, what he was asking . . . but she still couldn't imagine that anyone, especially his family, would be fine with what he was proposing. "You'd marry someone who was going to college? Who was following the way of the world? What would your parents think of that? Caleb, you'd be under the *Bann* for sure—both of us would be."

"My grandfather has a nurse who comes in, who helps my mother. They're not against accepting help."

"But will they accept help from me?"

"Will it hurt to try? To ask?"

"I would like to meet your grandfather . . ."

"And the marriage part?" Caleb removed his hat and tapped it on the side of his leg.

"*Vell.*" She tilted her head and looked at him. His face was close, and his eyes were intense. A beautiful blue color like nothing she'd ever seen before, shining with sincerity. "I want you to ask, Caleb. Don't mix up the question with your plans. Can you just ask?"

His hand went to the side of her head. She guessed her hair was a mess from the helmet, the ride, and the rescue, but she didn't care. He wove his fingers through her hair, and the intimacy of it tugged on her heartstrings. The warmth of his closeness and the tenderness in his eyes combined to make her light-headed—dizzy, even.

She felt like she was part of some romantic dream to find this man—this handsome, caring man—looking at her with such care. Her emotions mingled inside: hope, fear, worry, excitement. She clenched her hands, noting they were sweaty. What was taking him so long? A cool breeze hit her face, and her chest tightened, both from a chill and from excitement.

"Rebecca," he finally said. "Will you marry me?"

"*Ja*." The word burst from her. "That's the best part."

"Best part?" His brow furrowed in confusion.

"The best part of being swept away. Whether I liked it or not, I love where I've ended up. *Ja*, Caleb. Yes, I will marry you!" She wrapped her arms around his neck.

But even in the joy of the moment, worries pushed their way back in. "But will you be able to understand, Caleb, that it would mean a wedding outside the Amish church?" She pulled back and looked into his eyes again.

"Outside the Amish church, but in the sight of God . . . I believe I can work with that." He straightened his shoulders. "I've always been one to take a plunge on the wild side."

Caleb took the steps to the apartment two at a time. He couldn't wait to get to the door. To knock. To see her face.

Yet when he got to the top of the stairs and turned, he saw her door was already open. Rebecca stepped out wearing her jeans and a pink hoodie. The same ones she'd worn on the wagon ride. "I'm planning on wearing my Amish clothes when I get back, but the trains . . . Well, I heard they can be cold this time of year."

He rushed to her and swept her up. "I can't believe it's been nine weeks. It seems like nine years." He pulled her to him and she laughed.

"Honestly, Caleb, I'm not a log that you can just toss around like that."

"I know you aren't. I understand that. And I wish you would understand that my family will love you. They've heard all about you. And it's okay if you decide to wear a hoodie once in a while. I promise."

He released her and took a step back, noticing the uncertainty on her face. He didn't blame her. She'd grown up hearing about the same rules, living in the same system. But Caleb also knew that they had time. They would adjust, and they had God, who would help them out. He didn't need to talk Rebecca into trusting him. They would follow God—trust Him—and trust each other, together.

He entered the apartment, realizing that it wasn't much bigger than his room at home. She'd told him it came furnished, but even that was sparse.

"You can't keep me from being excited about our new life—and where it will be taking us both."

"I'm excited too. I hope your parents don't mind having me around." She flipped off the light switch in the kitchen and then glanced around as if resolving the fact that this season in her life was over. He took her hand and squeezed it. He really wanted to kiss her, but he respected her too much to do it here, now.

"No, they won't mind having you around," he said, stepping back. "They're eager to meet you. My sisters too. And . . . well, I've told someone else about you. He's heard everything, even about our days together on that wagon seat. It's probably more than *Opa* wanted to hear, but I know he won't repeat it . . . and he hasn't changed the subject yet."

She laughed.

"Do you have everything packed up?"

She nodded and pointed to one cardboard box and her suitcase. "Yes, everything's there."

"Ready to discover Ohio?" He lifted the box with one hand and then picked up the suitcase with the other.

"Yes, and I talked to the school in Canton. Everything transferred over fine. I'll be able to start at the beginning of the new year."

Caleb smiled at her. "It's a new life, Rebecca. A chance to be swept away together."

Epilogue

Most Amish brides didn't wear their dress outside their home until their wedding day, but Rebecca had a special mission. She walked outside of Caleb's parents' house. She'd slept last night in his childhood bed, and he'd slept in his sister's room. It had warmed her heart to picture Caleb as a boy. Of course he was a boy no longer. He was a man.

She walked onto his parents' porch and spotted him. His eyes crinkled with a smile as he moved to her side and squeezed her hand.

"You look beautiful, Rebecca."

She closed her eyes and let his words sink in. For so long she had let the wall around her heart guard her from getting too close, lest she had a change of plans. What she hadn't realized was that God's plans were even greater than hers, and that she *could* have the three things she desired: to be a nurse, to marry a good man, and to be part of an Amish church. The Amish/Mennonite church was different from the way she'd grown up, but she discovered they embraced her following, her calling, to be a nurse. She was thankful they'd be able to live with Caleb's family—at least until their own house was built on the property—and she'd be able to be a part-time caretaker to Caleb's *opa*. Someday she hoped to get back to Indiana, but until then she would walk along with joy on the path God had set before her.

Caleb led her to the small *dawdi* cottage set apart from the house. He pulled out a chair and she sat, only then looking at the man in the bed. *Opa*'s eyes were upon her. His face was a blank stare, but she noticed something in his eyes. Joy. And, yes, the hint of tears. She looked up at Caleb and he winked at her.

"I think my *opa* likes your dress."

"*Ja*." She looked down at it. "It's a bit fancier than one I'd wear at an Amish wedding, but I don't think I mind one bit. Yer mem did a beautiful job sewing it for me."

He took her hands into his, and Rebecca expected them to pray silently, but instead Caleb's words released in a voiced prayer.

"Dear Lord, *danki* for this woman, my bride, and for this man—my *opa*—who taught me to see life as an adventure. With her by my side I know I will. Guide us this day. *Aemen*."

When he was finished, she looked up at him. "I think Ben and Marianna are influencing you. You're praying out loud, I see."

"*Ja*, more than you might think." Caleb shyly looked away. "Ben and I have talked about every week or so since I left Montana. He'd been giving me advice about the marriage stuff. It seems it's more challenging than I thought."

Rebecca patted Caleb's cheek. "*Ja*, but you've always wanted a challenge, right?"

He nodded. "I wouldn't have it any other way."

It was then that Rebecca turned and took the hands of the man lying in the hospital bed. It took both of her hands to wrap around his large ones. They were weak now, and the skin was paper thin, but she remembered they hadn't always been this way. He'd once been strong and hardworking. He'd once run his farm and worked alongside his wife to raise a houseful of children. Holding his hands made her understand even more what the commitment she was making meant.

"In sickness and in health," she whispered to Caleb.

"Excuse me?"

"*Ach*, it's what the *Englisch* say when they get married. 'For better or for worse, for richer or for poorer, in sickness and in health . . .'" She sighed. "When I worked at the bakery I wrote those words on bridal shower cakes many times. I just had no idea then that those words could be for me."

"I like them . . . and they are for you."

She couldn't help but think about her *oma*, and she had a feeling deep down that her grandmother would have told her she'd chosen well.

"Yes, Caleb. Those words are for both of us. God has brought us together, and as we seek Him—trust Him—we'll live a life He's planned. And I have a feeling it won't be what we expected, but exactly what we would have chosen if given the chance."

Caleb took a step closer and wrapped an arm around her shoulders. He agreed with her. This was where they both needed to be. She had no doubt. No doubts.

Discussion Questions

1. Rebecca made a decision to become a nurse after her sister's tragic death. Why was that a hard choice for an Amish woman?

2. Caleb is always in search of adventure. How did adventure and risk-taking mask Caleb's inner struggle?

3. Marianna was Rebecca's friend who left the Amish. What surprised you about Rebecca and Marianna's relationship?

4. What did you learn about the expectations placed on men and women in the Amish community?

5. Caleb was first drawn to Rebecca because she was the only woman who looked away from his smile and antics. Why did Rebecca have a wall around her heart?

6. What character surprised you the most? Why?

7. What was unique about the relationships in the West Kootenai between the Amish and *Englisch*? How is this different than in other Amish communities?

8. Millie tells Rebecca that the word for "priest" in Latin is *pontifex*, which means "bridge builder." In what ways has Jesus been a bridge builder in your life?

9. Millie offered this advice to Rebecca on the trail ride: "Sometimes the best thing we can do with our minds and hearts is to allow ourselves to rest. After all, a heavy heart takes a lot of work to carry around." How did Caleb and Rebecca find "rest" in this book? How did it change them?

10. In what way were Rebecca and Caleb's unique gifts able to save the boy who fell off the bridge?

11. How did Rebecca and Caleb's trust in God grow in this story?

12. How did Rebecca and Caleb learn, as Millie said, that "truth is sweet"?

Acknowledgments

I am thankful for my friends who have shared the Amish lifestyle with me. Ora Jay and Irene Eash, thank you for sharing about your northwest Montana wagon train trip!

Thank you to Amy Lathrop and the Litfuze Hens for being the best assistants anyone can have. Many people ask how I do it all . . . Thankfully, I don't have to do it all, thanks to you!

I also appreciate the HarperCollins Christian team, my editor on this project, Sue Brower, plus Jodi Hughes, Katie Bond, Laura Dickerson, Daisy Hutton, and Becky Philpott. Your insight, help, and enthusiasm have been amazing! I also send thanks to all the managers, designers, copy editors, salespeople, financial folks, and everyone else who make a book possible!

I'm also thankful for my agent, Janet Grant. Your wisdom and guidance make all the difference.

And I'm thankful for my family at home:

John, it's amazing that we're about to celebrate twenty-four years of marriage. I love you now more than ever!

Cory, Katie, Clayton, and Chloe. I love having you CLOSE! God is good!

Leslie, I love your heart for God and others. Thank you for representing the Goyers on the other side of the world!

Nathan, I'm so proud of the man you're becoming. Keep growing in Him.

Isabella, Alyssa, and Casey. God gave us a wonderful gift in you. Thank you for bringing lots of laughter and lots of crumbs into my life!

Grandma Dolores, I am a blessed woman. Eighty-four years old and shining for Jesus!

And to the rest of my family . . . I appreciate all of you! I'm so thankful you're in my life! God gave me the gift of you!

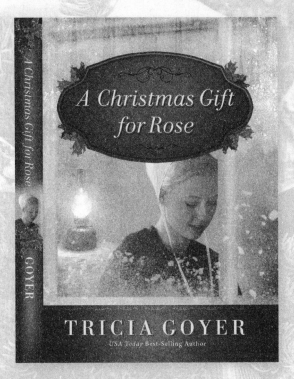

9780310335153-A

WITH HER HEART—AND
HER LOYALTY—ON THE LINE,
CAN SHE LET TRUE LOVE IN HER LIFE?

A SEVEN BRIDES FOR SEVEN BACHELORS NOVEL

◦ Available in print and e-book ◦

The garden plays a pivotal role in every Amish
household. Explore the different ways the
garden provides for four different women
in this new collection of Amish novellas
from Beth Wiseman, Kathleen Fuller,
Tricia Goyer, and Vanetta Chapman.

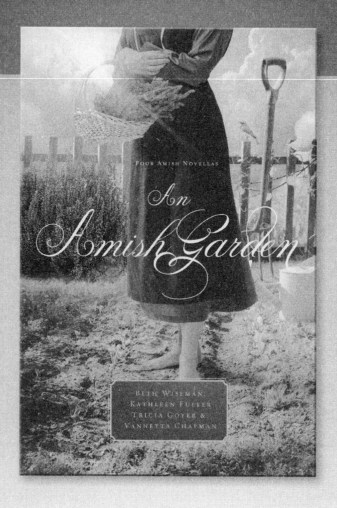

FOUR AMISH NOVELLAS

An

Amish Garden

BETH WISEMAN,
KATHLEEN FULLER
TRICIA GOYER &
VANNETTA CHAPMAN

AVAILABLE IN PRINT AND E-BOOK

9781401688707-A